Copyright © 2013 by Under the Redwoods Writers

All rights reserved. Except as permitted under the U.S. Copyright Act of 1976, no part of this publication may be produced, distributed, or transmitted in any form or by any means, or stored in a database, or retrieval system without the prior permission of the authors.
writersundertheredwoods@gmail.com
ISBN 9781493716616

Under the Redwoods
Six Women Tell Tales from Memory

•

Under the Redwoods Writers
*Christiane Diehnel, Nancy Dods, Judy Storey Edgar,
Anne Sisler Latta, Donna Terdiman and Janet B. Wentworth*

Contents

Authors' Note

Acknowledgments

- Stairway to the Past — *Janet Wentworth* — 1
- A Christmas to Remember — *Christiane Diehnel* — 9
- The Day It All Ended — *Judy Storey Edgar* — 17
- Pixie — *Donna Terdiman* — 23
- Leaving Home — *Nancy Dods* — 29
- Stateside — *Anne Sisler Latta* — 35
- Stealing Time — *Janet Wentworth* — 40
- Just a Minute — *Janet Wentworth* — 41
- 3 a.m. — *Anne Sisler Latta* — 42
- Each Morning with a Lovely Voice — *Judy Storey Edgar* — 43
- April 8, 1945 — *Christiane Diehnel* — 45
- Uffizi — *Donna Terdiman* — 53
- We All Have Basements in Our Lives — *Janet Wentworth* — 61
- Wind in My Hair — *Janet Wentworth* — 64
- Over the Years — *Anne Sisler Latta* — 66

• Genes at Work	*Christiane Diehnel*	68
• Working for the Witch	*Judy Storey Edgar*	71
• The Lady in the Red-Brimmed Hat	*Anne Sisler Latta*	79
• The Gum Tree	*Nancy Dods*	83
• The TR4	*Donna Terdiman*	89
• Veterans Day, 2011	*Nancy Dods*	93
• Socks	*Janet Wentworth*	95
• Locked Inside	*Judy Storey Edgar*	97
• Occupation	*Cristiane Diehnel*	103
• Mother's Kitchen	*Donna Terdiman*	113
• Lost	*Anne Sisler Latta*	122
• Memory Police	*Janet Wentworth*	124
• Decisions, Decisions	*Nancy Dods*	125
• Chap's Guitar Music	*Janet Wentworth*	129
• Whiskey Max	*Anne Sisler Latta*	131
• Turning Points in My Life	*Janet Wentworth*	140
About the Authors		143

Authors' Note

We met in a memoir writing class given by Jackie Kudler at the College of Marin and came together as a group to share our writing with each other – like fitting together pieces in a jigsaw puzzle.

We call our group *Under the Redwoods* because on warm summer days we often gather in a redwood grove in Ross, California. The trees muffle most sounds, giving us a sense of privacy and quiet in which to read our latest works. We try to delve into hidden and sometimes painful memories in the basements (and attics) of our lives, where, among the bric-a-brac, treasures are stored – priceless memories obscured by time. Brushing aside the cobwebs, we reveal our stories to ourselves and to each other.

We have come to trust one another to help shape our stories, and are proud to offer a few of them in this collection…our "stairways to the past."

Christiane, Nancy, Judy, Anne, Donna and Janet

Acknowledgments

We would like to thank the following:

• *Jackie Kudler*, for helping us to develop the skills needed to tell our stories, and for continuing to motivate and encourage us.

• *Janet Wentworth*, long-time member of the Lagunitas Country Club in Ross, who made it possible for us to meet there.

• *The Lagunitas Country Club*, for welcoming us to its nostalgic and inspiring setting.

• *Patricia Scales*, for her photograph of the six of us under the redwoods.

• *Jim Edgar* and *Tracy Morris*, Judy's son and daughter-in-law, for their time, effort, patience, and computer savvy in putting this book together.

"Mervor + Derry's House"

Stairway to the Past

Janet Wentworth

It was my late husband's idea to take a look at the Green Street house in San Francisco. "I've heard it's a mess. Maybe we could get it for a song and have it restored," he said. I wondered at the time, his being a New Englander, about his idea of "a song."

Ghosts and memories buried for years came back to me. As we trudged up the long flight of stairs leading to the front door, I asked myself, "Why am I doing this?"

At the first landing, I told him about the block bully. How he taunted me about my name, "Hervor." One day, my mother – exasperated by my timid attitude as the bully perched on the railing, laughing and daring me to pass – shouted from the half open front door, "Hervor, stand your ground!"

Thinking she might not let me in the door, I sidled up to him while smiling and said, "You're so mean!" And I simultaneously pushed him over the railing onto the neighbor's concrete landing. Crying, I then climbed over the railing to pummel him with my fists. We were thirteen. He was bruised, which upset his mother, who then called mine.

I became somewhat of a neighborhood heroine after that incident, if not a *bona fide* member of the Green Street Gang formed by a bunch of neighbor children while I was a boarder at Miss Wallace's School for Girls in Piedmont. Some fifty years later the Green Street Gang morphed into the Whiskey Hill Gang after my sister, then a widow living on Whiskey Hill Road in Woodside, married Art, a former Green Street neighbor, merging their two families.

More stairs to the front door. Its glass panel reminded me of another teen neighbor who chased me laughing up the stairs…until I slammed the front door on him, which could have left a piece of his face in the glass. Fortunately, it didn't, and the incident led to hilarious social banter years after he became a San Francisco attorney.

I unlocked the door. The front hall seemed shrunken without the familiar, large, gold-leaf mirror hanging over the green velvet couch. I didn't open the basement door, as I could smell memories of that dark place. Hearsay had it that there was a still in the basement during Prohibition. It was also where I'd hidden when I pretended to run away and could hear my parents calling the police.

The other door opened to the room where our Japanese cook, Nakka, and his "picture bride," Haru, our family maid, lived for three years. Their room had a slit view of the Golden Gate. My now-deceased sister once told me about the "cookie conspiracy" between Nakka and our mother.

"Nakka hid his home-baked chocolate chip cookies under his mattress, so you wouldn't get them," my sister told me. "Our mother worried about your weight gain." I found it hard to believe that a real live World War II spy lived there, let alone a retired Admiral, who would hide chocolate chip cookies under his mattress. The FBI whisked Nakka and his picture bride Haru off in 1940. Our family was sitting round the dining table one evening, having just finished dinner, when two FBI agents called on us. My mother offered them coffee which they declined and moved on to the living room to have a talk with my parents. They asked all sorts of questions including how long we had lived on Green Street, how long had my mother had her cook, and was he a good cook. My mother testified heartily to the cooking to which I silently agreed, having just consumed Nakka's chocolate soufflé. They seemed fascinated with Nakka's fishing schedule on his days off. They left soon after a politely requested tour of our house, amid much speculation by my parents. The following evening, which was not Nakka's day off, we had a pickup dinner in the kitchen. We never saw Nakka again. We later heard that Nakka – a retired Japanese Admiral – was considered a spy and exchanged for one of our prisoners of war. I have often wondered where my mother found Nakka, employment agency or personal reference?

More stairs to the second-floor living room that ran the width of the house. A fireplace framed by bookcases was on one end of the room. Facing the fireplace was a green velvet fire bench (now in my Sonoma home), where I listened to records on the antique six-foot-high Japanese Cherry Korean Chest, dramatized by shiny brass fittings (now in a nephew's Seattle home), that stood by the living room entrance. It was a family icon, given by Lillian Miller, world renowned Japanese American artist, shipped from Korea to my grandmother in the 30's. My parents had installed a phonograph and radio in it. A gleaming, seldom-used grand piano that my mother later gave to the San Francisco Symphony stood opposite the Korean chest. At fifteen, I wanted to use it. I dreamed of instant piano lessons, of pounding out jazz and popular tunes for admiring friends clustered around the grand. "Hervor, you have to learn the basics before you can really play at all. I don't think you have the patience," my mother often told me emphatically.

In the middle of the room was a row of windows overlooking neighborhood rooftops and the bay. A large couch with a coffee table in front of it stood under the windows, flanked by two chairs, one for my father. It was a special spot where my parents gathered for the cocktail hour. Feeling my history in the room, I had to tell my husband about my name change.

"This room reminds me of the large Christmas party my parents had when I was fifteen," I told him. By then, I'd had it with the Hervor name-bashing. My mother was a history buff and, according to her recently discovered notes, read Icelandic Sagas and other Viking stories and pulled the name Hervor from that ancient time. Who knows why. An older neighbor helped me draw up a petition where people could check their choice of three alternative names: Janet, Diana, or Phyllis. I left the petition on the hall table next to the living room entrance on a small table with an overhanging mirror. After also canvassing the block, the majority checked "Janet". I became Janet Bruce.

Separating the living room and wood paneled dining room was a large hall. The hall contained a phone closet and guest half bathroom.

French doors at the far end of the dining room opened to mother's pride and joy: a patio and garden designed by landscape architect Tommy Church, nationally known as the "California Gardening Guru" in the '40's to the '70's, complete with her touches as a talented gardener. A mirror at the other end of the room reflected the garden and a hand-carved antique dining table that mother had brought from England when they were first married. It seated fourteen when extended. Oil paintings of my great-grandparents, painted by my grandmother, Nellie Stearns Goodloe, an early California artist, hung on the wall. We had candlelit family dinners around that table. I remember peering shyly across the table at my date for a preteen dance school party when mother was trying – in vain – to engage him in conversation. During the war, we sometimes entertained enlisted officers on their way to the South Pacific. Mother, as was the custom then, usually dressed for dinner and cocktail hour in a hostess gown. I kept one of them, with a long train, though I can't fit into it. She kept a petite figure in spite of continuing orthopedic pain that might have originated from an old ski accident in Switzerland.

"If tables could talk," I tell my daughters when we occasionally gather around the smaller version (no leaves) of the same table in my Sonoma house. One story it would tell was the evening my hostess mother was late for her own 7 p.m. formal dinner party, missing the pre-dinner cocktail hour. Just as my worried father seated guests around the table, he heard a tap on the French patio doors. Mother burst into the room full of apologies, saying, "I have spent the last two hours in the next door elevator, because the neighbor's houseboy turned the elevator electricity off. I'm not sure he likes our arrangement …or me. I only got his attention by yelling and banging," she said. The "arrangement" mother referred to was a deal my father had made with the neighbor so that my once-athletic, now handicapped mother could share their elevator, and exit through a gate between their garden and ours. The elevator was installed when our neighbor's wife had to give up their stairs after her weight ballooned to more than two hundred pounds.

And still more stairs to the third-floor bedrooms. At the head of the stairs a bookcase marked a long hall, dividing two wings of bedrooms with a bathroom in the middle. My mother's and sister's bedrooms were next to each other on the garden-view side of the house. Mother remodeled that end of the house with architect Gardner Daily, in his signature style. What had been a porch off her bedroom was now glassed in so that the garden became part of the room. He designed a balcony with sliding glass doors overlooking the garden for my sister's large bedroom. Built-in closets lined the wall of mother's room. Her sleigh bed and decorative dressing table were covered in a brown-and-white wool type of fabric. I spent a lot of time in mother's room when she was out. I would spend hours trying on the contents of her built-in drawers and closets, sometimes "borrowing" an item. This led to certain amount of conflict… including being banished to boarding school.

Mother had great taste and my sister's room reflected her style. It was furnished with antiques and spool beds covered in a subtle blue and gray linen fabric. I loved her large airy closet with a window overlooking the neighbor's back door. That view became quite interesting at times.

All those stairs led to spectacular bay views for my father and me. Our bedrooms were next to each other. The decorator had enlarged the feeling of my little room by using mirrors and built-in furniture, gray walls accented with gray and yellow fabric, and a mustard yellow rug. I took this rug for accent color when I moved into my own home with my first husband.

To this day I wonder how that line holding a tin can suspended over the street from my room to my friend's room on the other side of Green Street was put in place when we were preteens. Was it her brother? I don't think our tin can, our first "cellphone," lasted for long.

The built-in bookcase under the window, running the width of the room, came in handy during the war. There I kept a copy of *Jane's Fighting Ships* and a pair of binoculars to see who, and on what ship, might be coming into the bay.

Father's room was larger than mine, with the same view, though it always seemed to me a little stark. Father's furnishings consisted of two spool beds – now in my Sonoma house – one large wing chair, a smaller chair and a freestanding, hand-carved frame mirror and matching antique bureau. Both the mirror and the bureau came from my mother's grandparents' old Tuscumbia, Alabama, cotton plantation home. Both those antiques are now in my younger daughter's Burlingame home.

On the bureau was a small mirror set in a frame topped by a silver angel that for some reason always represented my father. It was last seen in – of all places – the bathroom of my recently deceased sister's guesthouse. I cherish the picture and records of other memorabilia

Under the Redwoods

I've kept over the years. At this writing I wonder what happened to the World War I pistol that my father kept unloaded in the top drawer of his bureau. He showed it to me once as a relic of his time as an Army lieutenant on the front line in France. He never mentioned how – or if – he used it. I never asked.

Ours was a creaky old house, and one night as I was on the top floor and alone in the house at seventeen I heard a suspicious noise on the lower stairs. Remembering the unloaded relic gun, I thought I would scare an intruder. Pointing the gun down the stairs I hissed, "Tell me who is there or I will shoot!" My mother replied in a tiny voice, "It's your mother."

The old house literally had its ups and downs, but we had fun. My father enjoyed his sunny Sunday gin fizz brunch gatherings on the patio. I remember one particular Sunday when mother's friend Adele came for brunch with her husband, a high-ranking officer, escorted by two attractive young officers. I understood that he had headed the Alaska front during the war. The officers had quite a time guiding him down the stairs.

So much for stairs! Writing this is exhausting enough without living with them again, even for a "song." Thanks, dear husband, for the thought some forty years ago.

"View from 2535 Green Street"

A Christmas to Remember

Christiane Diehnel

My mother, my grandfather Opi, and I were hurrying along the lonely road on the outskirts of our City of Halberstadt in Germany. The December air was getting colder with the approaching darkness and made my feet and fingers tingle. All three of us were bundled up with woolen hats, mittens, scarves, and warm coats. Our winter boots made crunching noises every time we stepped on the frozen snow on the pavement. Those were the only sounds around us except for the occasional soft whispers exchanged by Opi and my mother. Around us were only snow-covered fields. There was no traffic. We saw no houses, no lights and there was no moon.

A vague black line appeared in the distance and grew bigger with every few steps. Soon we were close enough that I could see it was a forest. Opi said to us, "Stay here and wait for me to return. And be quiet. I won't be long, and as soon as I am back, we'll go home. Don't worry, it will be all right."

My mother did not say anything, just nodded her head, and held my hand a little tighter. Carrying the small handsaw he had brought, Opi disappeared in the forest and we were all alone on the road. It was the day before Christmas Eve of 1944. I was five. I remember that outing very clearly and still feel cold in my bones when I think about it. I was also scared and did not know why we were there. I whispered to my mother, "Mami, I am cold and I am scared. Why are we here and where is Opi going? I want to go home now."

This outing reminded me of the scary fairy tales I loved. My mother often read them to me when both of us were snuggled up in bed. However, I did not feel comfortable and safe out here on this cold night.

"We have to wait for Opi to return. He will be back in a few minutes and you don't have to be afraid. Let's stomp our feet and clap our hands. That will warm us up a bit."

We danced around each other and waved our hands and arms for a while but Opi did not return and my mother said, "I think we should slowly walk back before we get too cold. Opi will catch up with us."

"Mami, what is Opi doing in the forest, why could we not go with him?"

"I'll tell you a secret. Opi is looking for a Christmas tree for us. It is too dark in the forest for us to go with him. When we get home, we will all have some of the hot chocolate I saved for a special occasion."

"Oh, goody! I hope Opi hurries up and comes back very soon." However, he didn't and my mother mumbled that we better start back to the city, and hopefully Opi would catch up with us.

As soon as we set out, we saw a figure approaching us. My mother later told me that at first she thought it was Opi, but the figure got larger and larger and Opi was a small man. At that point, she felt scared because we lived in very unsafe times. The person coming toward us had spotted us too, and called in a booming voice in broken German, "Madam, not to be afraid, I not do anything. You waiting for man with tree? He looking for you, he way back there."

He was pointing toward the city. The man was probably Polish, one of many in the forced labor camps scattered around our area. Who knows where he was headed. I tried to hide behind my mother's back. My mother thanked him and wished him a Merry Christmas, which he reciprocated. We walked as fast as we could to where the man had indicated Opi was waiting for us. When we met him, Opi told us that he had quickly found a small tree he liked. In his haste to return to us on the road, he had gotten lost in the forest and had ended up farther down the road than he had planned. We were all relieved when we got home, especially my mother, I think.

In Germany, Christmas trees traditionally were put up only the day before Christmas. The children were not allowed in the living room to see the decorated tree before the celebration began in the evening of December 24th with the arrival of Santa Claus carrying a big sack on his shoulder with presents for the children. If Santa Claus was too busy and could not come himself, the presents would be waiting under the tree.

After the war, when my mother and I had joined my father in his home village of Lasbek, our celebrations began with my father lighting the candles on the tree after dinner. Then my brother Uwe and I took turns standing in front of the tree, each one of us reciting a Christmas poem we had memorized. Often we lost our concentration and forgot our lines when our eyes wandered to the unwrapped presents hoping to spot the one toy we wanted most of all.

My favorite Christmas poem was, and still is, one by Theodor Storm. It starts with this stanza:

Knecht Ruprecht
Von draussen vom Walde komm ich her
Und ich muss Euch sagen, es weihnachtet sehr!
Allüberall auf den Tannenspitzen
Sah ich goldene Lichtlein sitzen...

Santa Claus
From out there, from the forest I am coming
And I have to tell you, Christmas is near!
All over the tips of the fir trees
I saw little golden lights sitting...

Next, the whole family sang a few Christmas Carols, more or less in tune, and finally my father handed out our presents.

In my family, Christmas Eve dinner was always something quick and simple, like sausages with mustard and bread. We were all looking forward to stuffing ourselves later with cookies and candies, which were washed down with hot cider for us kids. The adults enjoyed Gluehwein (hot mulled wine) or Grog (rum mixed with sugar and boiling water.)

However, in 1944, when I was five, it was difficult for everyone to get into the holiday spirit. Most families would not be able to exchange many presents or enjoy the traditional goose for dinner on Christmas Day. Food and other necessities had become increasingly scarce. Many men were away fighting in the war, which seemed bleaker every week. My mother told me years later that Opi had decided he would make sure there was a Christmas tree in our home that year and that Santa Claus would bring me at least one present.

Before our expedition that December evening, Opi had scouted out the forest near the city where he could cut a small tree for us. This was not legal and he had talked my mother into going with him and bringing me along. His reasoning was that in case we were stopped by the police, he would use the excuse that we were on our way to visit relatives in the country. My mother did not like the idea, but finally went along with it and that's how she and I ended up on that lonely road in the dark.

I don't recall all the activities in our household the next day to get ready for Christmas Eve, but suddenly it was time to go into the living room to see our tree lit with a few candles. There were only the three of us, my mother, my grandmother Omi, and me. My mother told me that my aunt, Tante Motte, would come later and Opi had to work. My father and my uncle Helmut, Tante Motte's husband, had not been able to get leave from their respective military units. When the doorbell rang, my mother said, "Who could that be?" She went to open the door and called out to me, *"Der Weihnachtsmann* is here! He wants to talk to you."

Santa Claus stepped into the living room and looked around. He was wearing his red suit and pointed hat. His long white beard hung halfway down his chest, but he was not as tall as I had imagined. His back was bent under his bulging sack, which he put on the floor with a big sigh. He grunted as he adjusted his black belt over his big stomach while looking at me. I felt a little scared and clung to my mother.

"Christiane, have you been a good girl?" he asked me in a deep voice.

Timidly I managed to whisper something like Yes.

"Well then," he said, "I leave presents for all good kids and here is yours. Be a good girl and mind your mother. Then I will bring you another present next year."

He pulled a big box out of his sack and put it on the floor. As soon as he had done that, he asked Omi, "Do you have a bathroom I may use?"

Omi got up and showed him where the bathroom was. I did not know that Santa Claus had to use the bathroom like we did and there was something else about Santa Claus which puzzled me. I said to my mother, "Mami, why does Santa Claus talk like Tante Motte?"

"I don't think he talks like Tante Motte, it probably just sounds like it to you. Let's open the box and see what he brought you."

My present turned out to be an exquisitely made miniature grocery store painted red on the outside. Looking in through the open front, I saw that the walls were white and the counter and drawers blue and yellow. I discovered that the shelves and bins were stocked with real noodles, beans, candy, cocoa, flour, sugar, oatmeal, sewing thread, ribbons and many more things I could not all remember that fast. A little scale stood on its counter and a cash register with a drawer, which had pennies in it. I had never seen anything so beautiful and felt totally overwhelmed. I could hardly wait to show it to my friend Christel, so we could play with it together. She would be my customer and I would weigh and measure the things she wanted to buy. My mother put the store on a low table for me so I could easily play with it.

Santa Claus returned from the bathroom and hastily wished us all a Merry Christmas, reminding me once again to be a good girl before dashing out the door mumbling that he had to visit a lot more children that night.

Years later my mother told me that Santa Claus indeed had been Tante Motte. There had been no man to take on these duties, so she had borrowed the costume from friends. Santa Claus suits were not widely available in those times and my aunt's friends needed the suit back quickly to use it for their family and then loan it again to someone else, all on the same evening. The reason that Santa Claus had needed to use our bathroom was that the beard was sliding down and Tante Motte was afraid it would fall off, so she had to do some quick thinking to find a place to fix it where I would not see her. Our whole family laughed about this dilemma every time we talked about it for many years to come.

My grandfather, Opi, had wanted to make this a special Christmas for me and had spent many hours building the grocery store and everything in it with meticulous care to the last detail. After the holidays that year we took it to my grandparents' apartment to keep it safe in case our apartment building near the train station should be bombed. In the end, it was my grandparents' place in the center of the city, which was bombed and burned to the ground in April of 1945, and my grocery store with it.

Under the Redwoods

The Day It All Ended

Judy Storey Edgar

It was April 23, 1945. Mother arrived at the front door of our split-level suburban home just as I skipped across the living room and joined her, gleeful that I had mastered the art of perfect skipping. As she opened the door, responding to the high-pitched doorbell, she took a quick step backward and gasped, her hand to her mouth. There on our doorstep was a tall, young military officer holding his khaki colored brimmed hat in his left hand, a crumpled telegram in his right.

"Sorry, ma'am," he began, "but the orders were that you were to be the first one notified…"

I was shocked to hear Mother begin to wail. I knew something terrible had just happened.

Our Uncle Mort was dead.

Uncle Mort was our hero, our link to the unbelievable happenings in Europe which we knew of as World War II. As children, we did not know or understand the details of the war that was raging so far away, except that fathers and uncles were serving their country by leaving us, sometimes for a long time.

My sister Helen and I knew we had to clean our plates at dinner because of the starving children in Europe. We knew that Mother couldn't buy sugar and butter as she used to, and she shopped with ration books like all of our neighbors on Meadowbrook Road. We watched Mother pour cooking fat into large cans which she turned in for the red stamps she could use to buy meat. We crushed tin cans by stomping on them after the tops and bottoms had been cut off, and added them to the metal scrap pile which Dad carried to the street every week to be picked up for the war effort. Helen and I helped Dad with the work of the neighborhood victory garden at the foot of the hill, in which we'd planted squash, tomatoes, lettuce and beans to supplement our family's evening dinners. We knew we were good helpers.

Uncle Mort, Mother's unmarried younger brother, had finished school and lived for awhile in our dormered red and white guest room while he began his new job as a machinist for Western Electric Company, in the nearby town of Kearney, New Jersey. We loved listening to his deep voice reading the Sunday comics to us as we sat on either side of him, feeling his strong arms around us as he carried Helen and me up the stairs to bed some nights, and smelling the pungent smoke wisps of his cigar as he sat on the back porch smoking and discussing politics with Dad. He quickly became a much-adored member of our family.

Whether he was drafted or enlisted, I don't know. One day he came home dressed in a khaki and brown uniform.

"Wow, you look different!" I exclaimed, as Helen and I greeted him.

"You are now looking at a member of the Armed Forces of the United States of America," he told us proudly. "I'm headed for basic training at Fort Dix, in south Jersey."

"But we'll miss you," Helen said in a sad voice.

"Don't worry, kids," he said. "I'll come back to see you whenever I can."

And he did. We were very happy each time Mort was able to get a pass from the base and arrive for a weekend visit. Upon his arrival, Helen and I would burst out the front screen door and run down the flagstone path to the street to hang on his strong arms again. Dick and Georgie, the neighbor boys, would march over to greet him chanting "Hup, two, three, four." They tried out their newly learned salutes and asked to carry his duffle bag or his hat. We all plied him with questions about being a soldier.

Mort always laughed and said, "There's plenty of time to talk later. After awhile you'll all be bored with my stories."

Mother would be ready with wonderful meals for the weekend, especially for our mid-day Sunday dinner after church, when we'd enjoy Mort's favorite meal of roast lamb, mashed potatoes and peas, with ice cream and butterscotch cookies for dessert. I think Mother saved up her meat rationing coupons especially for these memorable weekends, and she loved making sure everyone was full before leaving her table.

"You're spoiling me, Sis," Mort would say, blowing Mother a kiss.

Later Mort told us stories about life in the barracks with his new buddies.

"You wouldn't believe how hard it is to peel a whole bucket of potatoes," he said. "It takes so long your hands get numb."

"But why do you have to do that?" I asked.

"It's called k.p. duty," he responded, "and everyone has to do it."

"Are you shooting a gun?" asked Helen.

"Yes, but before you can shoot a rifle, you have to learn how to use it properly," Mort said, in a more serious tone. "You have to prove you know how to clean it, disassemble it and use it correctly before you're allowed on the shooting range."

We shook our heads as though we understood everything he told us. He often talked to us as though we were grown up.

After Helen and I were tucked into our twin beds at night, we could hear Mother, Dad and Mort talking in hushed tones about war and the future as they sat in the living room listening to the latest war news on the large console radio.

"It's bad, isn't it, Mort?" asked Mother, a frightened tone in her voice.

"Yes," said Mort, "We don't even know how bad yet. We only get a small part of the news from the war zone."

Sometimes Helen and I climbed quietly out of bed and sat on the top stair step listening, but we could never make sense of what they were saying, and soon rubbed our sleepy eyes and tiptoed back to bed.

When Mort's training was finished, he was promoted and received his orders to report for overseas duty. He was proud and excited to be headed first to England and later to an unknown destination. Uncle Mort, who had never been away from the east coast, was headed for

Europe to join the Allied Forces. He would be a member of the first Army, 512th Ordnance Department.

"This is it, kids," he told us as he said his farewells to our family. "At last I'll be a real part of this war effort. The Allies are going over there to beat the enemy before they can do more damage, and we're going to win."

We all cried as he pulled away from the curb in his battered black Ford, but he was smiling and giving us the thumbs-up sign. And that was the last time we saw our Uncle Mort.

The telegram and the officer at our front door came later. Uncle Mort had been killed in a tank accident in Germany in the very last weeks of the war in Europe. He was awarded a Bronze Star Medal. He died on April 12, 1945, the same day as President Franklin Delano Roosevelt. The country mourned the loss of their beloved president, and we wept at the loss of our dear uncle. The war continued a bit longer, but the day we got the news about Mort was the day it all ended for us.

Under the Redwoods

Pixie

Donna Terdiman

We called him Pixie because he was tiny and magical. I remember coming home from school one day when I was in the eighth grade and saying, "Mom, can I have a parakeet? Everyone else has one. You can teach them to talk. Please, mom?"

My mother's response was less than enthusiastic. Our family's earlier experience with pets had not been promising. My parents had taken in a friend's dog years before. The dog had adored my mother, but had assumed its duty was to defend all members of the household, and did so by biting my friends. After the dog, we had a kitten briefly, but that episode ended with its being run over by a car. We now lived in a small tidy house in Queens. My parents had managed to fend off periodic pleas for another dog or cat from my brother or me, and were quite content to live without animals. We didn't even have fish.

"It's cruel to keep a bird in a cage," my mother argued. "Besides, it's a tropical bird. It will be fragile and difficult to take care of."

"A bird flying around and crapping on your head is not my idea of a great pet," my father added. "Who's going to clean up after it?"

"I will. All my friends have parakeets. They sit on your finger and are friendly and sweet, and you really can teach them to talk, at least some of them."

"How ridiculous to think that any creature that weighs only a few ounces could talk," my father scoffed. But he was already relenting and eventually convinced my mother to let me have a bird. Perhaps he sensed that with my brother soon to leave to go to college, we could use an addition to the family.

With a final proviso: "You, young lady, will be completely responsible for feeding the bird, and cleaning its cage and not letting it fly into people's hair," my parents consented. The three of us then made a grand expedition to the pet store to select a bird and cage. Choosing one bird from the chattering, technicolor selection was delicious agony. I finally settled on an exquisite little creature with aqua breast feathers and a patch of cobalt blue above his beak. I looked into his intelligent eyes and named him Pixie. Even my parents were smitten by his chirpy charm.

Pixie was cautious at first and sidled away from me when I put my hand into his cage, cooed at him, and gently nudged him on his tummy with my index finger to encourage him to use my finger as a perch. Parakeets are immensely social little creatures. Soon he enjoyed coming out of his cage on my finger, or on my mother's or father's fingers, for they were as entranced with him as I was.

A tiny mirror and bell hung in his cage. He would dance and strut in front of it, bobbing his head, knocking the mirror with his beak, chattering to his reflection. My father called it "dovening," and pronounced him a miniature Rabbi. In short time Pixie had the run of our large kitchen and dining area, only using his cage for eating and sleeping. He craved attention, would sit on your finger gazing intently into your face and listening even more intently to your speech. Gradually his chatter sounded more and more like human speech. We had been advised that to teach a bird to speak you must repeat one phrase over and over. "Pretty bird," I said to him again and again in a gentle sing-song. Soon I began emphasizing the sounds, rolling the r's until I sounded like a native of Glasgow.

My parents also tried to teach Pixie, but were both skeptical about his ability to learn to speak. Finally Pixie came out with it, an unmistakable "pretty bird" with a dense Scottish brogue. We were astounded. Total converts, my parents boasted to all their friends that they had a talking bird.

The next phrase we taught Pixie was a natural. Whether he was on your shoulder or perched on your finger, Pixie would lean forward passionately, his little body straining to reach your lips and kiss. He didn't need to be taught this. He seemed to do it instinctively. He learned to say "kiss me" relatively quickly and to suit the action to the words. He never bit us, and with his sharp little beak he could have done quite a bit of damage.

Because we had our meals in the small dining area of our large kitchen, Pixie was usually the center of our attention. My mother, so fastidious about her food, thought it was adorable that Pixie would march across her buttered toast to share it with her, or sit on the edge of her coffee cup and take a nip. We had a stainless steel toaster on a small chest near the table. Pixie would spend hours dancing up and down before this larger mirror chattering to the bird in the reflection. "Pretty bird," he would say. "Pretty, pretty, pretty bird. Kiss me!"

Once he mastered the first few phrases, Pixie learned very quickly. "I loove you," we would say, and in short order he would say, "I looove you," back. A definite rhythmic pattern was helpful for longer phrases. He would say, "I-am-a Dod-ger fan" in exactly the same intonation as he was taught.

Pixie had a small toy penguin, about an inch and a half tall and weighted at the bottom, that he loved to bat with his beak. He soon learned to maneuver it to the edge of the table, knock it to the floor, then lean over the edge of the table, cock his head and say, "Pick it up." How could you not? We delighted in picking it up only to watch him knock it off the table again and repeat his command. He delighted in his mastery of a new phrase, a new game, and in training us well.

Pixie craved human companionship. He responded to all sounds, particularly the human voice. He loved it when we were all in the kitchen and he had a choice of shoulders to perch on. He participated in the preparation of meals, hanging on to my mother's shoulder as she moved from counter to stove, clanging pots and pans while she cooked dinner, or literally looking over my shoulder as I cut up salad vegetables. He joined our dinner conversations, and reveled in the cleanup. He enjoyed the clatter of dishes and the splashing water in the sink, hopping back and forth and commenting all the while in his own language and ours. He loved the sound of the tea kettle and enjoyed a companionable cup of tea in the afternoon, with perhaps a bite or two of my mother's favorite tea biscuits.

He liked to sit with me while I practiced the piano, perched on top of the piano music, sometimes quiet, sometimes chattering away, often nibbling on the tops of the pages. Like a small child, he hated to go to bed at night. When I tried to get him into his cage, he would often fly to a curtain rod near the ceiling, watch as I climbed laboriously with his cage to the top of the kitchen counter, balancing my legs on either side of the sink so that I could hold the cage with its opened door to face him. He would wait just until I would reach him, both of us saying, "Time for bed, Pixie." Then he would flit across the room to the other curtain rod. "Pixie, you naughty bird."

"Naughty bird," Pixie would agree.

As time passed, Pixie's language became more sophisticated. "I am such a pretty bird." "I am an extremely intelligent bird." "I am very naughty." "Kiss me. Kiss me. I loove you so much." He learned all our names and would apply his own embellishments. Once, when some particularly soulful music was playing on the phonograph, my mother heard Pixie trilling to the music, saying, "Sweet, sweet Sarah." We had taught him "sweet," and we had taught him "Sarah," my mother's name. But he had put them together.

I think of this as his epitaph. He died of pneumonia shortly after. It was winter and he was a tropical bird. We had had him for only about a year. I mourn him still. I treasure the memory of this amazing little creature from the other side of the earth, and I treasure the munched pages of my music books.

Under the Redwoods

Leaving Home

Nancy Dods

"Nancy dear. It's time to wake up." Grandma softly patted my shoulder. "Smrf, snuffle," I replied.

I heard Grandma get down on her knees beside my bed. I could smell her perfume. It's Elizabeth Arden Blue Grass. She leaned ·over and kissed my forehead, then her fingers slowly brushed my hair from my face. I didn't want to wake up.

We were leaving today.

We were leaving Grandma's house. This house had been my home for 3 years while Daddy was overseas in Italy, fighting the War. I didn't like the War. I was afraid the Germans would bomb us and that Daddy would get killed. I had missed Daddy, but now I was mad at him for being home because now we were leaving. His new job was in a big city far away from Excelsior, Minnesota. We were going to Kansas City, Missouri. You had to lock your doors in Kansas City.

I had done my best to stop our move. Every time Kansas City was mentioned, I had a severe attack of asthma. I had to sleep sitting up in a chair, all the while gasping for breath. It felt like someone was sitting on my chest. No matter how deeply I took a breath, it seemed as if no air was going into my body. It was scary. I really didn't do it on purpose. It just seemed to happen. We were still going though.

I opened my eyes. Grandma was still looking at me. "OK" I said.

Assured that I was awake, Grandma left the room. Arey, my sister, was already up, dressed and ready to go. She was excited.

I rolled over and looked at the door that went from our bedroom on to the deck outside. It was a special door. It was divided into two pieces. You could open either the top or the bottom. If the top was open, I could lean out and see the leafy branches of the huge maple tree that was the geographic marker for Grandma's house – "You know, the big house on the hill with the big maple tree in the front yard."

I had gone out on the deck and eyed those branches many times. There was a thick one that came over the railing. I knew that my Uncle Oz had climbed across it and clambered down the trunk to meet his friends. Now I'd never be able to try that. I was only 8 years old. He was old, 21, I think. He was in the Navy.

On summer nights when the top door was open, I could hear the screams of the people riding the roller coaster at the amusement park at the edge of Lake Minnetonka. People from Minneapolis went there. They were lucky. We never got to go to the amusement park unless Uncle Stuart took us. Then we only got to go on the Merry-Go-Round or the huge slide with ripples in it. I went down the slide but the burlap sack we had to sit on made me go too fast and made my legs itch. For being so brave, Uncle Stuart gave Arey and me $5.00. He had a job and could give money away.

One night Mom came in.

"Girls, wake up! There's something you must see!" She opened the deck door and led us outside. The floor of the deck was cold. Even though it was night time, it wasn't dark. The sky was brilliantly painted with fuzzy streaks of red, and lavender and pink. It was the first time I had ever seen the Aurora Borealis. After that whenever I wanted to show off my artistic ability, I would get out my red, lavender and pink crayons and draw it. Everyone liked my drawings.

"Nancy. Get a move on," Daddy called.

Reluctantly, I kicked off my covers, sat up and swung my feet onto the floor. After fumbling around trying to find my slippers with my feet, I got down off the bed, knelt on the floor and looked under the bed. There they were, way in the middle. I lay on my stomach, reached as far as I could, and grabbed one, then used it to shove the other one out. I thought of the time Grandma stood in the doorway of our bedroom and said, "Would you please get everything out from under your bed, Nancy? I'm going to do a wash." I didn't move. She repeated it, again and again, each time more sternly. I finally got the stuff out. As I did, I stuck my tongue out at Grandma. I was between the beds, on the floor; my face was completely hidden. "And don't you ever stick your tongue out at me again!" Grandma said. How did she know?

Instead of going down the hallway to the bathroom, I went out the door to the deck and through the door that was "kitty corner" and that went directly into Grandma's room. I walked through slowly, trying to memorize everything. I touched the blanket cover on the bed. It was so silky. The times I sat on it as Grandma was braiding my hair so tightly that my eyes would water were seeming like good times. I wandered around touching the bottles of perfume on her dressing table, picking up her hairbrush, dabbing a bit of powder on my nose.

"Nancy, hurry up. Breakfast is ready," Mom called from the bottom of the spiral staircase.

Time was running out. I crossed the hallway to the bathroom. I loved this bathroom. From here, I could look out the low window to the street and see who was going by. I loved the feel of the hand towels with the bumpy material that was so stiff and white. They had Grandma's initials on them and had lace on the bottom. (One thing I could never figure out though. I used to watch Mrs. Dyer wash the clothes. She would pour a bluing liquid into the white clothes. Why did that make the clothes white and not blue?) I never used those towels because I didn't want to make wrinkles in them. Instead, I rubbed my hands on my dress. Today, I wiped my hands on the towel.

I got dressed and started downstairs. I stopped. I turned and went back to the top. I went back to our room one more time. I stood in the doorway and took a deep breath.

"Goodbye, Room," I said.

I turned and walked toward the stairs once again. I leaned over the railing. I could see the fireplace from there. It was from here that I saw something I didn't want to see. One Christmas Eve after the Midnight Service, Mom and Grandma came back with some friends for a "nightcap" and cookies. I heard them come home, got out of bed to see who was there. I looked over the railing. I didn't see a nightcap, but I saw my mother put a doll under my stocking which was hanging on the mantle. The doll had on red pajamas and a hat.

Mom was Santa. I hurried back to bed, put my pillow ever my head and cried. I acted surprised when I came downstairs that Christmas morning.

As slowly as possible I made my way to the back porch where everyone was eating their breakfast. The porch overlooked the woods and Mr. Sutton's back yard. In the summer we ate on the porch. I'd close my eyes and listen to the whispering of the leaves and the hooting of the owls. There was always a soft breeze off the lake that cooled everything. Those summer mornings we would have fresh berries with whipping cream and baking powder biscuits with butter and jam that Mom and Grandma had made the summer before. I wondered if our house in Kansas City would have a porch.

In the winter, the back porch was a place to dump our snow suits and boots. Mr. Sutton's back yard was the best hill in town for sledding. At the top of the hill, when I was on my stomach on my sled, I couldn't see over the edge. With a push of my foot, I'd drop over into eternity, speed along to the next level and another edge, off that one, down another long hill to the road that marked the end of Mr. Sutton's property. If I could make it across the road, it was a great ride. Mr. Sutton always had a fire going in an old oil drum outside his garage. We'd go there to warm our hands. At night he'd have cocoa and hot dogs for everyone. I don't think it snows in Kansas City. I don't want to leave.

It was time to go. The suitcases were all in the car. Grandma had packed things for us to eat on the trip. We walked down the front steps for the last time.

Under the Redwoods

Grandma knelt down and gave me a big hug and a kiss. I didn't want her to let go.

Arey started to cry. I started to cry. Mom and Daddy started to cry.

As we drove off, I looked out the back window and saw Grandma standing under the maple tree, waving. I watched until I couldn't see her anymore.

I wondered if Grandma was crying.

Stateside

Anne Sisler Latta

"Damned fascists!"

Mother angrily stubs out her Pall Mall in the overflowing glass ashtray and lights another, never taking her eyes off the television screen. The year is 1954 and I am a few days shy of being fourteen. We have just returned from a five-year tour of duty at Clark Air Force base in the Philippines and are temporarily billeted in a hot, horrid little house in Alexandria, Virginia while my stepfather awaits reassignment.

"Are you now or have you ever been a member of the Communist Party?" Joe McCarthy booms from the television set. Mother's eyes never leave the screen.

"Can you believe that bastard?"

She sits in one of two chairs liberated from the debris of dusty packing boxes. Since our return her complete attention has been on the hearings.

"Anzy, be a dear and run down to the market and get me another pack of cigarettes, okay? And better get some milk too while you're at it."

"Oh Mom, please, please, please don't make me go."

I hate this house – dark paneled walls, dun-colored rental furniture, sun beating through smoke-filmed windows, surrounded by the chaos of temporary housing – and I am terrified to leave it. This is my country, America, "stateside," where I have dreamed of being for years, where there is ice-cold real milk instead of powdered KLIM, real butter, real eggs, a new thing called television, 3-D movies, the latest music, swell clothes, hot dogs, ball games, snow. I am terrified to be here. This is not my country.

My country was so different. The people called it "Land of Light." It was a land where the sound of reveille woke you up and "taps" drifted across the soft evening air as the Stars and Stripes was lowered every sundown; where the sun rose early and hot; where sudden tropical downpours pounded on the tin roofs so loudly that conversation was impossible; where the houses had bullet holes in the walls – a reminder of not-so-long-gone days when this was a battlefield; where the earth could rattle and shake and we would all run across the street to the Parade Ground, Mother yelling at us to "grab the plates!" and we would stand on the vast open field clutching Mother's large Imari plates to our chests, watching the tennis court backstops whip back and forth through the air like so many syncopated fly swatters.

It was a land of friendly brown people who at dusk could be seen squatting down on their heels laughing and talking and smoking by their fires; where one could open the front door to tiny, black bare-

breasted men and women, Negritos, who wanted to sell their beautifully-crafted bows and arrows and who wandered the base freely – after all, it was their land – and who had been the fiercest of all guerrilla fighters during the war and of whom the Japanese had been terrified; where you couldn't go off base at night for fear the Huks would shoot you; where you couldn't go barefoot because of hookworm; where a typhoon could whirl in, tearing up nipa huts, and the swirling flood waters would come right up to the tops of the concrete piers holding up your house; where your gentle-voiced amah spent hours picking lice out of your hair until she triumphantly held up a small wiggling worm-like creature declaring "This is the mother of all lice"; where the fear that the Korean War would spread to us was ever-present as we listened to the great jets and transports roar in and out of the air field, picking up new supplies for the front and leaving behind their terrible cargo of the dead and the dying; where there were alerts and the base siren sounded much louder than any small-town noon siren because it could signal possible attack and we would all run to the bathroom and climb into the tub, Mother would throw a mattress over us and stand guard with a .45; where everyone believed that what they were doing was for the good of America; where all the children went to school together – blacks, Filipinos, Chinese, Malaysians, whites, Hindus. It didn't matter – we were all part of everything.

Our big dream was to return "stateside." New arrivals were met with countless questions about what it was like "stateside." "Stateside" became an almost mythical, magical kingdom to us. The very red, white and blueness of it all meant home.

After five years in the land of light we sailed home on the U.S.S. President Cleveland – my mother, stepfather, twin sisters, brother and Arsenio, an eighteen-year-old Filipino boy whom my parents wanted to send to school in the states. We kids must have stood on the deck for hours before the silhouette of the Golden Gate Bridge emerged from the horizon. It loomed larger and larger in all its majesty and for us, represented America. We sailed under it singing "California, Here We Come!" excited to see the San Francisco skyline – laughing and crying and hugging each other. We were "stateside" at last.

In San Francisco I had the tallest, coldest glass of milk possible; we went to movies to see 3-D, the family, like seven magpies sitting in a row, shrieking in terrified delight as "The Creature from the Black Lagoon" lunged through our cardboard sunglasses.

My parents bought a Chrysler limousine which we called "The Hearse." It had fold-down seats in the rear and could hold all of us. We crossed the country, ever vigilant for Burma Shave signs, listening to Doris Day crooning "Secret Love" on the radio until we arrived in Virginia.

And now, here I am in this wretched little house, which I hate, but which has become my fortress – my barrier against my native land. It doesn't feel red, white and blue to me. I have twenty-three days to finish the eighth grade. I take the public bus to school. I fumble through coins for the right amount and finally, in desperation, put a recognizable dollar bill in the coin box.

"Don'cha know what a quarter looks like?" the bus driver yells.

No, I don't. I don't know there *are* coins here in America. We had only used paper money, "scrip," overseas. I slink to a seat. I notice there are no Negroes on the bus – they are walking. Two white boys scream out the window of the bus "Hey Nigger!" and they spit.

I find myself standing up in a classroom full of surprised eighth graders whom I've never seen before, fists clenched in angry indignation, face hot with nervousness, expressing my horror at what I had seen, that such an event could take place in our country and why aren't Negro kids in school with us and didn't anyone care? The teacher is as shocked as everyone else. This is the South. This is not proper classroom discussion! Her eyes plead with me not to cause trouble, to be a good girl and sit down and not think about such things. One boy understands my anger – Norman Polowski. I decide I love him. I do not take the bus again.

I discover my beautiful new clothes made by the dark Hindu-eyed men at Mohan's during our three day stay in Hong Kong are out of date, I don't understand "stateside" slang or know how to dance, or what the "Hit Parade" is, what the latest movies are. Most of all, I don't understand how one American can spit on another.

"Mom, please, please don't make me go out."

"What's happened to you? Get yourself out there, make some friends, it's not good for you to always be in the house. You're going to have to get used to things here, Anzy."

Am I? I don't want to go out of this horrid little house. I want to lose myself in a book. I want to ignore the fact that I am now "stateside." I don't know where "stateside" is. I want to go home – home to the Land of Light.

Under the Redwoods

Stealing Time

how to live longer
what the scientists
attempt to define

turtles live the longest
they have a shell
turtles can hide
when life is hell

turtles move slow
because they know
fast won't last.

Janet Wentworth

Under the Redwoods

Just a Minute!

minutes like pennies
add up
a day, a week, a month
a life time fortune

just a minute
to send that email
life time to live with it

just a minute to
to say I do
a life time to live
with him or her

just a minute
to conceive a child
a life time to live
with him or her

just a minute
to write this
dumb poem!

Janet Wentworth

Under the Redwoods

3 a.m.

Thoughts running round my mind in
ever decreasing circles
Guinea Pigs clutching, scrabbling
on a tiny wheel
leading to more thoughts.
A mind,
set on redial.

Oh, for the bliss of whiteness
The blank page where my thoughts
do not appear
The contest I do not enter
The life I do not judge
The silence I do not fill

Perhaps, there, in the
space of no thoughts
a soft whisper of wisdom might brush
past my heart
gently stroke my brow
The only sound
my steady breathing,
A lullaby.
I can sleep now

Anne Sisler Latta

Under the Redwoods

Each Morning with a Lovely Voice

she sang, as a child,
like a simple songbird,
perfect pitch
luscious in its sound.
Singing in the shower
singing as she dressed

sounds soaring
through the house
sending shivers through all who listened.

Now a young woman
turning twenty-one
singing with a symphony,
Juliet's Waltz.
"She's amazing, fantastic,
she's special," they say.
I rejoice, listening
to the crystal clarity
of her voice,
a joyous treasure,
my granddaughter's voice.

Judy Storey Edgar

Under the Redwoods

April 8th, 1945

Christiane Diehnel

Most Germans did not realize yet that the war and the nightmare of 12 years of the Nazi regime would be over in a month. The government and economy were collapsing, but war was still raging on all fronts. The Russians were closing in from the east, the Allied Forces were pushing forward from the west, but Hitler's propaganda machine continued to predict the Final Victory. Nobody had a clue as to what was really happening. Rumors about the daily changing war fronts and casualties could not be verified. Loved ones fighting on the various fronts had not been heard from in months. My father and my favorite uncle Helmut were among them. The daily struggle to survive meant standing in line for hours to buy bread, meat, milk, and whatever other food may still be available by the time a customer was tended to.

My mother and I had moved in with her parents whose apartment was in the center of the city. We thought to be safer there than in my parents' apartment near the main train station. So far, our city of

Halberstadt had been spared major damage, although the city was in the flight path of Allied bombers on their way to Dresden and Berlin. The frequent air raids day and night had been sending citizens into their basements or bomb shelters for years. In every household, a small suitcase containing a few basic items of clothing, family papers, and valuables sat by the door, ready to be grabbed on the way to the bomb shelter as soon as the air raid sirens started. Years later, my mother told me that she had gotten sick to her stomach after every air raid. The stress of not knowing if we would survive yet another air raid was too much. Opinions differed about the safety of bomb shelters capable of accommodating thousands of people. Many feared that a stampede would break out if a shelter took a hit causing people to panic trying to get out. Therefore, some preferred to take their chances of survival in their basements.

I was five and a half years old in April of 1945, too young to understand all of the circumstances the adults were facing. I learned them from my family when I was older. However, I have very clear memories of the events of Sunday morning, April 8th. My mother had gone to the store to pick up my allotment of milk. On her way back to my grandparents' apartment, the sirens started, it was almost 10:00 a.m. As she opened the door to the building, she could hear the drone of bombers. My grandparents and I were already on our way down from the 4th floor. We all hurried to the basement for shelter, together with the other occupants of the apartment building.

At first, it seemed that the bombers were just passing over our city like so many times before, but suddenly there was a loud noise making the building shake. Not knowing exactly what was happening,

I was only a little scared. What could happen to me? My mother and grandparents were right there and they would protect me. Then we heard a boom, a second one followed a moment later. The candles we were using were extinguished by the air vacuum created by the impact of a bomb nearby. It was totally dark in the basement.

Some of our neighbors who were huddled close to us began moaning, praying, or screaming in fear. My mother threw herself on top of me. Her mother threw herself on top of both of us. My grandfather, hovering over all of us, kept repeating, "What is happening, what are we going to do? Who is going to help us?"

His words were lost in another explosion nearby. I was squashed on the cement floor and I remember that I could hardly breathe with the weight of my mother and grandmother on top of me. That tender spot on my belly hurt, too. A few months earlier, I had been ill with acute appendicitis, but since the local hospitals were overflowing with wounded soldiers at that time, I could not be operated on. Our family doctor, who practiced homeopathic medicine, had instructed my mother to put boiling hot compresses on my belly and administer his special medicines. During the worst days, he had come to check on me every few hours. Miraculously I had recovered quickly after the fever was gone, but in my mind my belly had remained tender for a while.

"Mami, my appendix hurts, you are squashing me," I cried.

"I am sorry," she whispered with a shaky voice. "You are okay. Don't worry, all will be well."

By now there was fine dust seeping through the cracks in the walls and door, making everyone cough. What was happening outside?

Had our building been hit? Nobody could tell. My mother put a handkerchief over my nose and mouth to keep the dust out, but soon our eyes were stinging, too. Would we be buried alive under tons of rubble from the apartment building? Would anyone come looking for us? Or would we eventually just die? Those must have been the thoughts going through the adults' minds. An hour and a half later, the planes were gone and quiet returned. It was over and we were still alive.

Someone called from above. My grandfather managed to open the door to the stairs going up and one by one we left the basement climbing over the rubble on the stairs. Our building was standing, but all the houses around us had been completely or partially destroyed. Dazed people were clambering out through the debris. A few nearby houses were burning, there was rubble everywhere. The beautiful old Martini Church across the street was partly damaged, too. We heard later that it had gone up in flames the next day. A man came running and shouted, "Around the corner all the buildings are gone, and everyone is dead!"

Hearing this, my grandmother screamed hysterically, "Oh no, my daughter is dead! My daughter is dead! I want to die, too!"

My mother's sister, my Tante Motte, lived in an apartment building around the corner. My mother put her arms around me tightly. My grandfather, trying to calm my grandmother and my mother, called to us, "I am going to check, you all stay right here. I'll be right back." With that, he ran around the corner.

The block warden, in charge of keeping order during bomb raids in this area, came by shouting, "Everyone has to leave the city in the next ten minutes. Everything is burning and there is only one street left leading out. Go, run fast!"

In another few minutes, my grandfather returned pulling my dazed aunt by the hand. He had found her alone, walking back and forth in the basement thinking that we were dead. She said she did not want to live either in that case. The tearful reunion only lasted for a moment until we heard more shouts to leave the city.

We hurried in the direction the block warden had indicated, dodging burning debris falling from buildings, whole walls collapsing, scorched trees with body parts hanging from branches, bodies in the street. Someone running by yelled to be careful because there was a lot of napalm on the streets. My mother lamented that she should have brought sunglasses for me so I would not have to see this horror, but all she had was the can of milk she had bought that morning. She tried to tie a handkerchief over my eyes, but I pulled it off. Many years later, a friend sent me a book about Halberstadt. In it was a photograph of a painting depicting the burning city on that morning in April 1945. The details of the inferno were exactly as I remembered them.

When we were finally out of the city, we found ourselves on a country road leading to several small villages. As far as the eye could see, a column of women, children, and old men stretched on that road fleeing the burning city. My grandmother was recovering her take-charge attitude and suggested we walk to the village of Harsleben where her sister Emma lived with her husband, Max, a cobbler.

It was normally about a two-hour walk, but on this day it took much longer. We refugees had hardly time to catch our breath before we heard the ominous drone of planes again coming straight toward us. The noise of the airplane engines became deafening as they dove down close to the road and started to shoot at us. The planes were flying so low, we could see the pilots in their cockpits. In panic, people jumped into the ditches on either side of the road. My mother spilled the milk she had so far been able to save for me. I don't remember how many times the dive bombers returned, and I don't know how many people were hit. Eventually we made it to Aunt Emma and Uncle Max's house where we stayed until the war was over in early May.

Halberstadt, in the State of Sachsen-Anhalt, is called the Gateway to the Harz Mountains. Historical records indicate that a permanent settlement existed at the site of the present city as early as 200 AD. In 804 AD Charlemagne declared Halberstadt a diocese. During the next ten centuries, the city survived various wars, infernos, the plague, and witch hunts. It was left with an extraordinary historical legacy in the form of many churches, Gothic architectural treasures, and extensive collections of medieval art.

In 1945, the city was home to more than 40,000 people. After that last air raid, all the splendor was gone. There were only burned out buildings, ruins, and rubble on the streets. Few people were about, and it was eerily quiet when we returned in May. Much later, we learned that during the last bomb attack 85 per cent of the old city had been destroyed and thousands of people had lost their lives.

My grandfather had ventured to the city alone a week after the bombing and had reported that my grandparents' apartment building had burned to the ground. My parents' apartment near the train station was damaged when the building had been hit by a couple of bombs. He thought he could fix our apartment up enough for us to live there. He had already started to secure the front door and put cardboard on the windows. He also told us that the apartment had been ransacked during our absence. Most of our clothes were gone, especially my father's.

After Germany had unconditionally surrendered and the war was over, we all returned to Halberstadt to begin our new lives amid the destruction that greeted us. When my grandmother stood in front of the building where she and her family had lived for many years, she looked at the burned out shell for a long time and then said with a sigh, "Everything we owned was in there and it is gone. All the hand embroidered pillow cases and table cloths, silverware, our family papers and photos. We don't even have any clothes left."

After a moment of reflection, she continued, "But we are alive and together! And now we don't have to polish the silver anymore. One less thing to worry about. Let's get going, we have things to do."

Under the Redwoods

Uffizi

Donna Terdiman

On Monday, July 4, 1960, our third and last day in Florence, Eileen and I turned up at the Uffizi Gallery first thing in the morning, in order to be there when the great doors opened. Perhaps that is why I found it so difficult to believe that the doors were not going to open. No one was there. It was Monday. The Uffizi is always closed on Monday.

"But, but," I spluttered, "our guide Franco told us he deliberately didn't take us here on our first two days so that we could come on our own today and spend as much time as we wanted. How could he not know that the museum is closed on Mondays? Why would he lie to us?"

Eileen shrugged. "I don't know. It's a shame, but I guess we'll have to do something else today."

"Something else?" I nearly shrieked. "Leave Florence without going to the Uffizi and miss seeing Giotto? Never." I had been pleased when our Florentine guide had suggested that we all go to the Uffizi without him. On our first two days in Florence, I had found him superficial and condescending. I was sick of his vapid tidbits from Vasari's *Lives of the Painters*. I really wanted to commune with Giotto alone. But tricking us into missing the Uffizi and Giotto altogether: this was unforgivable.

Less than three weeks earlier, I had stood with my fellow passengers crowding the deck of the SS Olympia, deliriously waving goodbye to my family in the festive crowd on the pier below. With horns tooting and banners flying, the great ship steamed out of New York Harbor for its ten day voyage across the Atlantic, past Gibralter, into the Mediterranean to the Port of Naples. I was 20 years old and couldn't believe I was actually going to experience Italy, to see the Blue Grotto and the Roman Forum, the ruins of Pompeii, and the canals of Venice, to eat pizza, and find out if Italian men really pinched your bottom. And I would get to Florence, to the Uffizi Gallery, and to Giotto.

I was a history major with a special fondness for the Renaissance. The previous January, in the middle of my junior year, I transferred from Mount Holyoke College, in Massachusetts, to Barnard, in New York City. My transfer cut short a wonderful course in Renaissance history. With a limited choice of courses starting in the middle of the academic year, I elected to take a course in Renaissance art at Barnard. At first this seemed like a major mistake.

The instructor was a spinster who wrapped her long thin body in the same long, thin cardigan at each class. She droned on endlessly, her repeated "ums," "errs," and "ahs" providing the only variation in pitch. But when I began to hear what she was saying, I was fascinated, and the slides were glorious. I loved the luminous images in that darkened room: Bellini's dreamy, distant landscapes; the angel wings of Fra Angelico; Fra Filippo Lippi's deep blue robes with decorated edges of filigree gold; the experiments in line and perspective in *The Battle of San Marino*; Botticelli's long willowy figures in their flowing drapery.

Most important of all, she introduced me to Giotto. "In a single room in the Uffizi Gallery," she intoned, "you can witness the transformation of European art from the Medieval to the Renaissance. On the left side is the painting of the *Madonna and Child* by the Florentine artist Cimabue in about 1300, still in the stiff, formalized style of the Byzantine era. On the right is Giotto's *Madonna in Majesty*, painted just a few years later, but showing a realistically seated mother tenderly holding her child on her lap, her rich blue robe molded and draped over her knees."

I loved roaming through the Renaissance collections at the Metropolitan and the Frick, but longed to see the masters at the Uffizi, especially Giotto. Then my parents informed me that they planned to go to Europe that summer. "We're going on a tour," mom said. "You can come with us if you like, or perhaps you'd rather go with people of your own age."

She didn't need to make that suggestion twice. Jumping at the chance to find a student tour, I found one that seemed perfect: a small group of students, traveling by ship to and from Europe, and within the continent by minibus and train. We would be staying in cheap and charming inns, rather than stuffy hotels. Our leader, Peter, was an Englishman barely into his thirties. Most important of all, we were starting off by spending three whole weeks in Italy.

Under the Redwoods

On the ship, I had tried to convey my enthusiasm for Renaissance art to any of my new friends who would listen. Eileen had been the most receptive. We had arrived in Naples full of expectation, amazed at the beauty, the sun, and the warmth of the people. Our timid "buon giorno's" were met everywhere with a flood of friendly Italian, which none of us could understand, but we learned to respond by smiles and hand gestures. We made our way north to Tuscany, and at last arrived in Florence.

We had three whole days. I was enchanted. We spent the first two days exploring the city on foot and on tours to various other galleries and palaces. We saw the Duomo and the Baptistry, Ghiberti's bronze doors and had climbed the magnificent Campanile designed by Giotto, taking endless pictures at every level of the splendid views of Florence and the surrounding countryside.

As we stood in front of the closed doors of the Uffizi, I was filled with rage at the cynicism of the guide. "I'm going to find a way to get in anyway," I announced to Eileen. As the rest of our group wandered over, and then wandered away to do something else, I roamed around the perimeter of the building – it looked like a fortress – searching for another way, any way, in. I finally found a back door, and using my eloquent hand gestures, convinced a guard to let me in, and to lead me to the director's office.

The director explained in beautiful Italian, I think, that the museum was closed today, and that I should come back tomorrow. I spoke in high pathetic, a combination of English, a smattering of Italian words, and many gestures, explaining that I was with a student group, that we were leaving Florence the first thing in the morning, and that nothing in all the world meant more to me than seeing Giotto's work in the Uffizi. Couldn't he please, please let me in? At last he seemed to understand. He handed me a form and led me to believe that if I got it signed at the American Consulate, he would let me in today.

It was now late morning and getting hot. I consulted my map. The American Consulate was a healthy walk away. Eileen, waiting outside for me, decided to do something else with her day. For me there was no choice but to make for the Consulate. After a long, hot walk, I arrived to find our American representatives in Florence celebrating July 4th. They invited me to join the party. They offered me hors d'oeuvres, and a whiskey sour even though I was not yet twenty one. All I wanted was to get my paper signed so I could get back to the Uffizi. Various people told me in the friendliest possible way that the Uffizi was closed on Monday. "But the Director told me I could get in today if I got this paper signed," I pleaded.

"Really, I've never heard of that," said one dubious functionary. But eventually he found someone to sign my paper. Before I left, I did use their restroom. I can report that the American consulate had the only decent toilet paper in Italy.

It was well into the afternoon as I took the long trek back to the Uffizi. Now it was really hot, and my feet hurt. But I was feeling triumphant because I was sure that now I was going to get in. I used the same method to gain entry through the back door and into the Director's office. He seemed pleased that I had gotten the paper signed. Next came a long bit of Italian, in which I understood only one word: "domani," – tomorrow. "Domani," I gasped. "I thought I explained I needed to get in today." Unfortunately I couldn't remember the word for today. No matter. The Director was busily explaining with satisfaction that because I now had a student pass, I wouldn't have to pay to get into the Uffizi tomorrow. I could not get in today, he explained with a sweet smile, because the Uffizi is closed on Mondays.

I finally accepted that there was to be no Uffizi for me. I went back to the hotel and told my sad tale to Peter and the group. Our festive last dinner in Florence was a wash for me. I could barely hold back the tears.

The next morning at breakfast, with all of us packed and our baggage in the bus, Peter announced that he had surveyed the group and everyone had agreed to leave two hours late and cut short our time in Sienna so I could get to see the Uffizi. The others thought they might as well come along too. I was overjoyed.

As I entered the first room I tried to force myself to be a student and look at the Cimabue first, but I could barely glance at it before approaching Giotto's *Madonna Enthroned*. "Look, Eileen," I whispered, "you can see that there is space behind her and the baby on her lap and all the angels around her." Now I looked at the Cimabue. How flat it looked, as if this Madonna and child and the masses of angels were painted on a plate. The expression on her face and the folds of her gown were rigid as metal, while Giotto's Madonna looked like she was really sitting with her gown, in my favorite midnight blue, draped softly and naturally between her knees. I couldn't take my eyes off her and continued to marvel at the tender way she gazed at her baby, and the naturalness of her figure. Eileen decided she'd like to see some of the other paintings in the gallery.

By the time I forced myself to leave, I barely had time to run by the other masterpieces, but I remember Simone Martini's *Annunciation*, Ucello's *Battle of San Romano*, Botticelli's *Birth of Venus*, which we called "Venus on the Half Shell." I knew the group had done this for me and in the bus on the way to Sienna I told each one of them, and Peter, how much it had meant to me.

Forty years later, in the year 2000, I returned to the Uffizi. I guess my student pass is no longer valid. The Uffizi is still closed on Monday. We planned our four day visit to Florence carefully, calling ahead from Vernazza to make reservations for the Uffizi on a Wednesday. This time, there was plenty of time, enough to go through the whole collection twice. The Giotto and Cimabue paintings are still in the same room. This time I explained the progression from Medieval to Renaissance to my husband Joe. When we went into the next room, however, I knew something was missing. "Where's the Simone Martini?" I demanded of the guard.

"It is being cleaned, madam. It will be gone for some time, I'm afraid," the guard replied. They speak English in the Uffizi now. I was disappointed at the empty space where the Simone Martini should have been. It was like missing an old friend.

On this second visit, I had as much time as I wanted to commune with Giotto and Leonardo, Botticelli and Bellini. But I missed other old friends. I remembered the thrill of that first hurried visit, and immense gratitude toward my traveling companions who had made it possible. The warmth of friendship, like the magic of the masters, lasts far longer than forty years.

Under the Redwoods

Under the Redwoods

We All Have Basements in Our Lives

Janet Wentworth

It is hard to believe it is the year 2000. I have been evacuating the basement of a building in Cow Hollow San Francisco – in the family since 1903. The old basement of crumbling memories and foundations has yielded some revealing facets of family history.

In one dark corner there were four large antique trunks. Way back then they were probably considered snappy steamer trunks. Inside one of the trunks was a wooden box containing a pile of letters written by my mother to my grandfather, as well as other letters between my mother and father. There were even some letters written by my grandfather to his daughter. I glanced at one letter from father to daughter written in 1912 in which he cautioned her that she was a little young at and inexperienced at 17 to "go around the world."

In another trunk, I first saw a whimsical oil painting of my mother in a blue dress as a child, painted by my grandmother, Nellie Stearns Goodloe. Later it hung in a room next to my now-deceased sister's bedroom in Woodside, CA. More current was the file I found on my son David.

Soon after we were married in 1964, my now deceased husband, transported newspaper files from the days when he was publisher of the Daily Tribune at South Lake Tahoe to the Filbert Street basement. As I thumbed through his filing cabinets, the David Scott Keast file jumped out at me. Titles of news clips in his file read: *S.F. Youth Killed in Cycle Mishap. Janet Thorn Wentworth's Son Killed in Mt. Rose Crash.* The story of his death ran in the San Francisco Chronicle, the Nevada State Journal, the Sacramento Bee and the Tahoe Daily Tribune. Condolence letters from the Navy and the White House and President Lyndon Johnson were in his file. David served on the U.S.S. Ticonderoga during the Vietnam War. There was a letter from his commanding officer in the file informing me that my son had a posthumous promotion to the rank of Aviation Machinist's Mate Third Class. David would have found that hilarious, considering that one of his favorite sayings was "Everybody has class in his class." I found other condolence letters that I had never answered – some of them heartrending. Many of the letter writers have since died. David would be 64 this year.

Memories of my son's life came flooding back as I flipped through the dimming papers. He was a mischievous little boy, doing things to get attention…like carving his initials on my favorite antique desk. I treasure what I can see of those fading initials now. There were episodes when I faked anger. One quiet Sunday morning on our dead-end street that bordered the Presidio wall, I answered the insistent ring of our doorbell to face a tall, thirty-something furious red-faced man.

He yelled, "I have been washing my Porsche for the last hour, and every time I think I have it clean, dirt appears. I saw two boys drop from the tree and run into your house. I should call the police." I found David and his visiting cousin, both 12, hiding in the garden bushes.

"Sorry Mom, if we got you into trouble, but it was fun…that is, until he looked up!" my son explained to me. "It was a super TV comedy – watching this guy wash and rewash his car as little pieces of dirt fell from the tree."

There were faded pictures of David as a choirboy at Cathedral School for Boys on Nob Hill. David had a scholarship there in return for my public relations work for the fledging school.

At 3 a.m. one morning on 54 6th Avenue in San Francisco, I heard David slip out of the house. I followed him in my car as he walked a few blocks through the dense morning fog to the Richmond Police Station. Frightened, I confronted him upon his return home, at 4 a.m – too early for his Chronicle newspaper route.

"It's okay, Mom, the police are going to take me to school and watch over me," he reassured me. "I told them I had been enlisted in a secret meeting the night before by some of the newspaper carriers who had planned to rob a sporting goods and gun store on Clement Street this morning." He had a police escort to Cathedral School for Boys on Nob Hill for several weeks after that.

A special David expression, (adopted from his stepfather whom he loved dearly): "You are so tragic-que," when any member of the family seemed to take themselves too seriously. It soon became a family saying and is today.

Under the Redwoods

Wind in My Hair

"where is your helmet"? "I don't care"
I want the wind in my face
and through my hair

he sat in front of that Reno bank
his motorcycle engine roaring

"I don't need a helmet/to hell with it
being the law"

I want the wind in my face
and
through my hair

discharged from his navy ship
he had driven his cycle from San Diego

we saw him soaring
around the sharp curves
of the mountain
as we followed in
our little mustang
the wind whipped through his hair
reddening his happy face

Under the Redwoods

why a cycle?
we had asked desperately

*"I want the wind in my face
and through my hair"*

the wind was blowing
over his face and hair
he lay still
on that fatal hill

*Janet Wentworth
7/20/98*

Note: David, my son, age nineteen had just returned from Vietnam on the U.S.S. Ticonderoga.

Under the Redwoods

Over the Years

How many times have we not spoken to each other
or spoken but left so much unsaid.
The mind takes over
parading ancient grudges across our vision
by the wheelbarrow,
shutting out the heart

Fear starts low down
gnawing at an empty belly.
We keep weaving a web,
a cache of shared memories
we have with no one else,
a shimmering thread
tenuous, but unbroken

I miss you
I miss myself with you
You make me laugh straight from the gut
Nothing polite.
Raucous
Uncensored

Under the Redwoods

You shot me full of arrows
dipped in poison, I thought
I pulled myself into the rock of myself
And wept

But when you told the truth
I felt loved.

Anne Sisler Latta

Under the Redwoods

Genes at Work

Many years of loyal service
Now we have to part
What will replace my Volvo?
Research, test drive
"Wait," says husband
The Cautious One
Scary new territory for me
The Independent One
Patience is not my forte
My Dad would know

Craigslist, Blue Book
TV ads, newspaper ads
Friends' advice
Sons' advice – opposite opinions
Certified pre-owned – what is that?
Hybrid, miles per gallon
Maintenance Costs
Honda or Toyota
Space for dog and Costco
My Dad would know

Under the Redwoods

Money in bank, decision made,
New blue Honda SUV
"Wait," says husband
"Used is better" says older son
"Let's buy your car today"
Says younger son
Stepping up to the plate
His grandfather's genes at work
My Dad would know

Christiane Diehnel

Under the Redwoods

Under the Redwoods

Working for the Witch

Judy Storey Edgar

"This is where you girls will sleep," said Mrs. Anderson, as she opened the battered wooden door of the small shack at the rear of the property.

She was a pale young woman with watery blue eyes and an air of uncertainty about her. She shrugged her narrow shoulders apologetically and stood to one side as Kay and I entered the building.

Inside the small room stood five cots and five orange crates, one crate next to each bed. Several bare light bulbs hung from the ceiling, a metal chain hanging from each one. A single dusty window at the back of the building let in a small amount of light. A small bathroom containing a shower, toilet and sink stood near the entry. It had no door.

I turned in dismay and looked at Kay, my best friend. She had a disappointed look on her face. This was not the kind of room we'd expected as the promised "room and board".

"Three more girls will be joining you," went on Mrs. Anderson in a soft voice. "They'll be here tomorrow. They're coming from Coatesville, Pennsylvania, out in the farm country. I'm sure you'll all get along just fine together."

With that, she gave us a hopeful glance and hurried toward the large white house where she lived with her husband and his mother. The house was a seashore inn, which served guests breakfast and dinner daily. It was named The Modauson – a contraction of "mother, daughter, son" – by the Anderson family, who owned the place. Kay and I had been hired as waitresses/kitchen help for the summer.

Kay turned to me and sighed. Then we both began laughing, with tears in our eyes, at our situation.

We had come to Ocean City, New Jersey, for a weekend about a month before, hoping to find a glamorous summer waitressing job together, and had ended up here. We had pictured ourselves in short black uniforms with starched white aprons, balancing trays with ease as we graciously served tables. Mother had driven us down from Chatham and had waited patiently in the car as we approached the famous seafood restaurants in this resort town, one by one. We heard the same story at each place: "We're only hiring eighteen year olds and older. Come back in a few years." We were sixteen, and becoming discouraged.

Then, as we drove around the residential area of Ocean City Gardens, we had seen the inn on a large corner lot, surrounded by a grassy lawn and bright red hibiscus bushes, only one block away from the wide south Jersey beach that we loved. The inn was painted white with green trim, and had tall pillars supporting an old-fashioned wraparound veranda studded with rocking chairs and a hammock. We had knocked on the door and met the younger Anderson couple, who showed us the spacious dining room with its deep blue walls and tables clothed in white linen. We were offered room, board and tips. The pay itself was meager. We would work breakfast and dinner, and have the middle of the day free. We took the job. It never occurred to us that they might be desperate for help.

Now we had returned to begin our job. We looked forward to meeting the elder Mrs. Anderson, picturing in our minds a plump, motherly innkeeper who would be delighted to have us there to help her run this charming place.

As we were being introduced to her the next morning, we quickly realized our misconception. The old lady stared at me, narrowing her steely blue eyes. She was short and wiry, with graying black hair pulled tightly back in a bun, a few stray gray hairs poking out in places. She raised her pointed chin when she spoke, as though trying to intimidate the listener. She reminded me of the wicked witch of the west from "The Wizard of Oz."

"You girls had better be on your toes all the time," she shrieked at us. "I expect you to follow our rules explicitly regarding everything from serving sizes to work hours. There's to be no argument over any of my orders. Do you understand?"

Kay and I shook our heads up and down in unison. It was clear who ruled the roost. The younger Andersons had stepped back and busied themselves in the kitchen as his mother spoke. Their eyes remained focused downward. They both looked extremely uncomfortable as she continued speaking to us.

"You!" she barked, pointing at me. "You don't look very strong to me. Can you carry a tray with plates stacked on it?"

"Oh, yes," I answered, "I'm sure I can."

Annoyed, she looked away and said, "Well, you'll have to do. Summer is here and we'll soon be busy."

Later that day, the Coatesville girls arrived, completing our contingent of five young waitresses. Kay and I quickly decided that they were extremely unsophisticated, as they exclaimed over our cramped living quarters, calling the place "cute as a bug in a rug". They marveled over the long strip of printed cotton fabric Kay had found at the local Five and Dime Store. We had tacked it up over the opening to the bathroom for privacy. They called it "fancy". They did not appear to have brought any books with them, and therefore had no problem with the lack of reading lamps, a fact which had annoyed Kay and me. As it turned out, we had nothing in common with them, and spent no time with them outside of working hours.

The next day our work began. Kay and I were excited about having a real summer job, although I was a bit wary about our situation. In addition, I was somewhat tired and weak. Before starting the job, I'd been a delegate to the National Conference of Student Councils in Chicago, and had traveled with other students for 19 hours each way on a bus. Our schedule had been grueling, and we'd spent most of our free time there in lively discussions. I hadn't had much sleep. Upon my return, I'd headed to Ocean City right away, without a break.

A couple of weeks into the job, I had my first real run-in with "the witch," as Kay and I now called her, over a breakfast serving. A woman who appeared to be nearly thirty was staying at the inn with her elderly parents, and they all came down to breakfast together on their first day there. They were plain looking people, and approached their table in a tentative manner. I noticed right away that the young woman was extremely overweight and had a sad look in her eyes.

"Good morning," I said, greeting them and smiling as I approached their table. "We have some wonderful blueberry pancakes this morning, as well as fresh fruit and the usual eggs and bacon."

"I'll just have black coffee and a piece of melon," said the woman, as her parents ordered a larger breakfast.

I returned to the kitchen and began to cut the melon. We had been carefully instructed to get at least ten pieces out of each cantaloupe. The pieces were tiny. It embarrassed me to serve something that small and charge the prices the inn charged.

Returning to the dining room, I served the table. The woman looked up at me in shock.

"Is that all I get?" she asked. "You know this is my whole breakfast. I'm on a strict diet to lose some weight."

"That's the size we serve," I said apologetically.

"Well, then, I'll have to order a second serving," she said, an annoyed tone in her voice. Her parents looked on with pained expressions.

I returned to the kitchen, and this time cut a larger piece of cantaloupe, feeling sorry for the hungry patron. She didn't look very happy to me. Just as I was leaving the kitchen to return to the dining room, the witch approached.

"What do you think you're doing?" she exclaimed angrily as she saw the serving in my hand.

"I'm serving cantaloupe," I replied.

"Don't get fresh with me, girl. You didn't follow my instructions about serving sizes."

"But, Mrs. Anderson, this is all that this guest is having for breakfast. Our servings seem too small."

"I'll make the rules here. Go cut that in half, and don't argue with me."

Her angry gaze followed me for the rest of the day, and I hoped I wouldn't lose my job over such a silly thing as a piece of cantaloupe. From then on, she watched me like a hawk.

A couple of weeks later, an incident occurred which made my future as a waitress there uncertain. Standing in the kitchen of the Modauson early one morning, I suddenly felt light-headed. The next thing I knew, I was on the floor looking up at faces, including that of the witch. I had fainted, for the first and only time in my life. Everyone was showing concern. Kay put a dishtowel as a pillow under my head and handed me a glass of water. She patted my arm.

"I knew from the beginning you weren't strong enough for this job," accused the witch.

"What happened?" I croaked.

"You fainted and hit the bench on the way to the floor," said Kay, holding my hand.

"Are you all right?" asked the younger Mrs. Anderson timidly, a sympathetic expression on her face. She stood by the large kitchen sink as she folded some ice cubes into a towel.

"I think so – but I've never fainted before."

"There's always a first time."

The witch surveyed the situation, and barked, "Everyone back to work. Judy – you go lie down. Everyone else will have to handle extra chores to cover for you. I'll talk to you later."

Since my family was vacationing in Ocean City at the time, I called and told them what had happened. They insisted that I have blood tests done, which indicated anemia. The doctor said I was exhausted, probably the result of my Chicago trip, and urged me to quit the job. I hated to appear weak and let the witch win, but at the doctor's urging and that of my parents, I considered it.

The witch had already decided. The next day she called me into the inn.

"I've lined up a substitute for you, another friend of the Coatsville girls."

"I'll leave, if you think that's best."

"You definitely should leave. You're just not cut out to be a waitress," she huffed.

I left, and spent the next two weeks with my family at their beach apartment. Kay and I still spent our mid-day hours together, lying in the sun working on our tans, our bodies covered in Coppertone. We ate hamburgers smothered in catsup and drank Cokes we bought from a fellow named Jack at the beach shack. Kay was torn between wanting to earn some money and her loyalty to me. She lasted another few weeks at the job, then quit, finally fed up with the work situation.

"Well, our first job wasn't exactly a stellar success," she observed.

"No," I answered. "I guess we'll have to say that it was a character-building experience!"

We looked at each other and laughed.

Under the Redwoods

The Lady in the Red-Brimmed Hat

Anne Sisler Latta

There is a place where the road rises up just before descending into the hollow of Olema. Looking right, one can see the sheen of Tomales Bay sliding all the way north. The sad half light of the November afternoon gives the hills and fields a muted sepia tone like a photograph you might find in your grandmother's attic.

I had come here to grieve. I felt I'd been cracked open like an egg and my innards had fallen splat on the earth far below. I was looking for beauty here, some piece of God, *anything*, that would reach into me and let me know that it was good to still be alive.

The sepia was fading to black when I arrived at Jerry's Farm House, built not long after the Civil War and painted barn red. Its porch extended across the front and the windows glowed yellow in the dark. There was a line of chattering couples and groups out the door waiting for a table. I joined them. I had almost made it to the young, long-haired hostess with glinty, dangling earrings when there was a tap on my shoulder.

"Are you alone?"

I turned. Her blue eyes perked up at me from under the brim of a Christmas-red baseball cap, silver permed hair sticking out on either side of her face. Her red jacket glowed in the light.

"We'll get a table faster if there are two of us. Let's have dinner together."

In five minutes we were seated in one of the crowded warm rooms in the warren of the old house, which buzzed with friendly noise and the clinking of glasses.

"My name is Bella. What's yours?" And then, "Well, Anne, what brings you out today?"

So I told her. I told her what had been pouring out of me to my friends, my therapist, and even, just after it happened, to a totally strange woman sitting next to me on the Jitney all the way from Sag Harbor to 68th Street in New York. I told her that my beloved second husband, the man I thought I'd finally found that I could rely on, who charmed me, who charmed my friends with his bigness, his spontaneous joie de vivre, his wisdom, his generosity, his love, turned out to be a swindler who ran a Ponzi Scheme on me, my family, my friends, some of my clients. All of my feelings of being loved had been false, had been based on an act, an act of treachery.

"The worst part is I still love him." I took a breath and a gulp of wine. "You don't stop loving someone because he's done something heinous. No one understands this. It's like driving a car at 60 miles per hours – when you slam on the brakes it's not an instant stop. It takes time to slow down no matter how much you want to stop." I looked at her expectantly.

The lady in the red-brimmed hat listened to all of this. After a moment she said "My husband of thirty years ran off with my best friend of thirty years. They're in L.A. so I came up here to be near my son."

I reached across the table to touch her hand, ready to commiserate, to share more.

"But," she said, "I'm not going to let what they did define the rest of my life. I'm moving on and putting this in my past now." She picked up her wine glass and looked at me.

She sounded so enlightened, so wise. I felt somewhat rebuked. I'd intended to continue my story, hear more of hers but this stopped me.

Then she said, "May they rot in hell."

I was so surprised I started to laugh and sprayed my mouthful of chardonnay across the table.

"And your husband can rot in hell, too!" She started to laugh and we laughed until tears came out of our eyes, slapping and banging on the table and spraying chardonnay.

"Do you like to sing?" Without waiting for an answer she got up, grabbed her wine. "Come on."

We sat in the hanging swing on the front porch, the light from the dining room window shining on our backs. We started with "Ohhhhhh, Oklahoma where the wind comes sweepin' down the plain." We went on to "The hills are alive with the Sound of Music," "Whatever Lola Wants, Lola Gets," "Bali Hai", "Gonna Wash That

Man Right Outta My Hair and send him on his way," "Ol' Man River," we steered clear of "Can't Help Lovin' Dat Man," but went for "Thank Heaven for Little Girls."

Friendly people went in and out of the front door; no one seemed to mind the two ladies swinging and singing on the porch and we didn't care. We both had clear voices and could carry a tune and best of all, knew all the words. We sang out into the night unfurling our flags of independence like two mocking birds, switching songs and rhythms at will. We ended with "Luck be a Lady Tonight. Luck, if you've ever been a lady, Luck be a lady tonight!"

We set our wine glasses down and took each other's hands. We held on for a minute looking at each other, and then she disappeared into the darkness of the parking lot.

I never saw the lady in the red-brimmed hat again. But I've never forgotten that winter's evening. Was she an angel? Was I *her* angel? I don't know, but she reminded me that somehow we get through. I'd like to say I've forgotten my sorrow, but I haven't. It's been many years. I mourn a little still, not for long, maybe fleeting, but it's there. And I always hear her words, "I'm not going to let what he did define the rest of my life!"

And then, a small, impish voice says, *"May he rot in hell."*

The Gum Tree

Nancy Dods

Mom looked at the clock on the kitchen wall. It was almost 3 o'clock. Arey and Don, Nancy and all the grandchildren would be here soon.

It was Saturday, which meant a family dinner at Mom's and Dad's. Mimi and Boppa, as they were called, loved having all the children around. They loved it when Nancy and the kids came from San Francisco. They relished all the laughter, noise and confusion that Arey's three and Nancy's three children created. The grandchildren were stair steps. This year Steven was 11, Suzie, 10, Sarah, 9, Laura, 8, Scott, 7 and finally Walter, who was 4.

"It's time to wake Ed up," Mom thought.

She wiped her hands on the embroidered dish towel and took off her apron.

She bent over and checked the third drawer down for spice drops. Filled. She mentally checked off the menu: chuck roast marinating, done; potato salad in the icebox, done; tomatoes sliced and sprinkled with sugar, done; cucumbers and onions in sour cream with dill, done; rolls made and rising, done; corn on the cob shucked, done; deviled eggs, done; apple pie and ice cream, done. This time she'd bought the ice cream instead of cranking it in the old freezer because she and Ed always fought while they were making it. There were not going to be any arguments today.

Satisfied that everything was all set, she headed up the curving back staircase, pausing on the landing to look out the window. She thought how quiet the house was with just the two of them. "Good. No sign of the predicted rain," she muttered to herself.

Daddy was sleeping in the sleeping porch, the long narrow room that went the width of the house and had windows on three sides. It had been the bedroom of choice for Arey and Nancy in the summer. With the breeze but without the bugs, it was almost like sleeping outside.

Jane hated to wake Ed. He'd worked all morning cutting the grass, trimming the edges and sweeping to make the yard as perfect as it could be for the grandchildren. Since he'd had his second heart attack, he seemed so fragile.

"Ed", she said loudly. No response. As always, when this happened, she checked his breathing to quiet her fear.

"Ed." Once again, nothing. Then, "Edwardo." His eyelids fluttered. Mom breathed a sigh of relief. Finally, "Ralph!" His eyes flew open. Daddy answered to many names, depending on Mom's mood, but "Ralph" meant "I mean business!"

"The kids will all be here shortly. Better get up, dear."

He smiled, snuffled and stretched. His legs felt heavy as he lifted them over the side of the bed. As he sat there in his skivvies, you could see on his uncovered arms and legs the psoriasis that had plagued him for so many years. Unconsciously, he reached down to scratch.

"Don't scratch, Ed," Jane said for the hundredth millionth time. She leaned down and kissed the top of his head. "See you in a few minutes."

He stood up, turned and looked out the window at the backyard. "Looks pretty good," he said admiring his own handiwork. He shifted his eyes to the towering elm that straddled our yard and Mrs. Shaw's. The trunk was on her side, but the branches, all leafed out in their summer splendor, were on our side.

"Tonight's Gum Tree night," he chuckled.

Suddenly, the quiet of the afternoon disappeared. The front door flew open and what seemed like 95 people came barreling in.

"Hi Mimi. Where's Boppa?" the kids yelled as they made their way to the kitchen. They headed straight for "their" drawer, reached in and each scooped up a handful of spice drops.

"He's getting dressed. He'll be down in a few minutes," Mimi replied.

As if on cue, Boppa made his entrance. His white hair was neatly parted and shining. His sweet smile made his eyes twinkle. And he was dressed in his usual sartorial summer splendor: tan linen Bermuda shorts, a polo shirt, with the top of his tee shirt showing in the vee of the neckline; a brown belt surrounded his thickening waistline. And to top it all off, knee high black socks and loafers. He wore sock garters only with long pants, thank goodness!

"How about a game of croquet?" Steven yelled. "You're on", Suzie said.

The rest of the kids trooped outside to play and pester.

The adults retired to the patio, since the bugs weren't out yet. They sipped their gin and tonics. They chatted; Daddy and Don talked about business as usual. Arey, Mom and I covered everything that had happened since we'd talked that morning. It was a storybook summer afternoon.

Boppa fired up the barbeque. Mimi brought out the chuck roast. Boppa, armed with his watch and his squirt bottle filled with water, put the roast on the grill and the drama began. If a flame appeared, wham, it met its end with a pull of the squirt bottle's handle. At five minutes, Boppa turned the roast. This continued until the Taylor meat thermometer (Boppa sold Taylor products) registered medium.

Mimi stood at the ready with a platter. Boppa whisked the roast off the grill and onto the platter with a look of triumph. Then Boppa, brandishing his special carving knife, sliced the succulent piece of meat into thin slices of perfectly done rare and medium steak. After Mimi had put every thing on the table, she went to the porch door and yelled, "Le diner est servi." The kids dashed into the dining room, while we followed in a more sedate fashion.

In a bit, Mimi asked, "Has everyone had a sufficient amount to satisfy their appetite?" Everyone responded with loud grunts and groans.

Out of the blue Boppa inquired, "Did you kids know that we have a Gum Tree in the back yard?"

"Aw, c'mon, Boppa," Steven said. "What's a Gum Tree?"

"Most trees produce acorns or seed pods, but the tree in the back yard produces gum," replied Boppa.

This was really unbelievable because we all knew that Mimi passionately hated gum (she also hated the word hate) because most gum chewers chewed with their mouths open and cracked their gum. Everyone was forbidden to chew gum in Mimi's presence. How ironic that a tree in their yard was there to annoy Mimi.

"You're pulling our leg, Boppa," Suzie said.

Laura looked at Mimi. "If it does, can we keep the gum?" Mimi just looked at her with her "are you kidding?" look.

"Follow me," said Boppa, standing up and heading for the elm tree. He looked like the Pied Piper with the six children following closely behind. He stopped about 10 feet from the fence. He looked up. Shielding his eyes with his hands, he squinted.

"Ah, I see some," he said seriously. Immediately, six hands went up to their eyebrows. Mimicking Boppa, they squinted. No one saw anything.

"Boppa, you're teasing us."

"No, I'm not. Just because you can't see something doesn't mean it's not there," he said. "Do you want me to show you?"

"Yes" the kids shouted.

"First, each one of you must find a special rock. It might look ordinary to someone else, but it must be special to you," Boppa instructed. The children scurried around searching, searching until each one had that special rock.

Boppa stuck out his hand. Each child put his special rock in it. Boppa took a couple of steps backward, stopped, looked up. He moved a little to the left, looked up again, then moved to the right.

"This is the right spot," he announced solemnly. He took a deep breath. He put his hand on his hip. He reached into his pocket for his handkerchief, took it out and wiped his brow. He put his handkerchief back in his pocket. He took another deep breath. The children held their breath.

He swung his arm back as if he were a softball pitcher and brought it forward fast, releasing the special rocks. Spellbound, the children's eyes followed the rocks. All the rocks looked the same as they flew skyward, disappearing into the leafy canopy.

Nothing happened.

Suddenly, it sounded like rain falling on the leaves. There was a loud gasp as little squares of Chiclets came showering down. It looked like an Easter Egg Hunt as the children raced around trying to recover as many of this forbidden fruit as they could.

Steven is 44 years old now, Suzie is 43, Sarah, 42, Laura, 41, Scott, 40, Walter, 37. Between them, there are eight great grandchildren. These great grandchildren have all heard this story. They have never seen it happen. But they believe it. It is a legend. After all, Boppa performed his magic innumerable times. The grandchildren have all tried it, hoping beyond hope that this time the gum will fall. Boppa never told anyone the secret. The secret died with Boppa.

The TR4

In 1964, young, sleek,
dressed in virginal white,
she zigged and zagged
through New York's angry traffic,
ignoring geometry,
proving
that the shortest distance
between two points
is not
a straight line.

"She can stop on a dime,"
Joe boasted.
But once,
the dime
turned out to be
Charlie Jenkins' bumper.

She took us on noisy,
exhilarating rides:
Chicago, David's birth;
Bethesda, Cindy's birth;

Under the Redwoods

the Badlands
and Yellowstone
to California.

When a hole in her floor
revealed the freeway
hurtling
inches below our feet,
she was banished
to the garage.

In middle age: a makeover.
Her engine rebuilt,
clad in sizzling
metallic red,
she became cool
and sexy once again.

Our teenagers
abandoned
the stodgy station wagon,
learned to shift
her flamboyant gears
and roar
around the neighborhood.

Under the Redwoods

Always a Prima Donna,
She demanded constant attention.
Without it,
She stopped running,
retired to the garage.

The cats
made a home
in her upholstery.

On her sad red hood
our firstborn
wrote with his finger,
"Help! I'm stuck
under all this dust.
I need to get out."

That was 25 years ago.
The dust
and the TR4
have not moved.

She sits like a dowager queen,
surrounded by her musty court:
cartons and old furniture

Under the Redwoods

piled to the ceiling,
broken plastic containers,
ancient skis, soccer balls, tennis rackets,
lathe and radial saw,
one hundred thousand screws.

Like the Lionel trains
of his childhood,
Joe has not forgotten her.
One day, he will restore her
to youth and beauty,
free her
from his fetid garage.

Now and then, he reminds me,
with a wicked smile,
that before he fell for me,
he was already smitten
with his TR4.
"You're lucky," he adds,
because I never give up
on the battered old things I love."

Donna Terdiman

Under the Redwoods

Veterans Day, 2011
Fredericksburg, Texas

Like Tombstones

Rows of chairs line the grassy hill

Slowly, like a grave yard
Each chair is occupied
Uniformed dignitaries
File past the rows
Medals sparkling
The Colors are brought in

Uniformed cadets

March down the side aisle
Backs straight
Weapons on shoulders

Guest speaker, a Chaplain
World War 2 veteran
Shares his story
He lost both legs
Each war is named

Under the Redwoods

Applause accompanies
As each veteran stands
Cadets ready their guns
Fire an 18 gun salute
I wonder

Could this happen in San Francisco?

Nancy Dods

Under the Redwoods

Socks

warm socks
curled up in my
drawer

cold today
I think I will
wear them

Thanksgiving
and Christmas
you were gone

you died
in March
left me alone

only Bruce
to tell our
story

our children
and grand children
generations to come

Under the Redwoods

thanks for the socks
cold today
I think I will wear them

clouded years
dementia overcast
with childhood
memories

your heart
reached out to me
only sister

warm socks
cold today
I think I will wear them
I miss you!

Janet Wentworth

Locked Inside

Judy Storey Edgar

CLANK!!

The thick steel bars of the heavy gate slam down behind me. I stand in a no-man's land, facing the second set of bars that serve as the inner entrance to San Quentin Prison. A rush of fear suddenly hits me, and I shiver and lick my dry lips as I wait. After a few long moments, the second gate begins to open. I am chilled by a feeling of helplessness. I've been warned by the admitting guard what to expect, but standing here between two immobile barrier doors is frightening. The guard has also prepared me with a few rules.

"Once you're inside, you're there until we let you out. If there's any kind of violent disturbance inside, such as a prisoner uprising, we go immediately to lockdown. You will not be able to leave," he said.

"I understand."

"Don't attempt to respond to any prisoners' comments as you walk in. Eyes straight ahead until you reach your destination."

I pass through the second gate, a guard on either side of me. On my left is a sixty year old San Quentin veteran, red-faced and overweight, and on my right, a short, muscled young African American woman. They both pack weapons, and their faces are unsmiling. A heavy odor of disinfectant permeates the hallway, which is dark gray and musty. Far down the hallway ahead of me, a man in an ill-fitting blue jumpsuit mops the corridor. As we pass him, I can see the open interior courtyard, which is empty. There are four small windows facing the area and a series of hallways leading inside to the cell tiers. A few prisoners are gathered at the end of one hallway close to the courtyard. As we pass by, two of them begin to shout.

"Hey, Blondie…come on over. I got room in my cell for ya."

"Yo…didja come to see me? I been waitin' all day."

Bawdy laughter and an undercurrent of murmuring voices follow the comments, and I remember the rules: eyes straight ahead, no reaction. We walk through another long damp corridor before we reach our destination, a meeting room that will serve as my classroom.

It's 1982. I've been at my job as a program executive with the San Francisco Foundation for less than a year. One of my responsibilities is to present bi-weekly workshops for community members and non-profit agencies on how to apply for a grant from the Foundation. The workshops are intended to inform and assist those who hope to get financial support for their projects. During each workshop, I explain the process of submitting a letter of intent, which, if encouraged, will lead to the submission of a full grant request. I always list exactly what information has to be included, emphasizing the importance of being specific and concrete in the description of the project. Then I answer and discuss the many questions that inevitably arise.

Recently a request has come in from the warden at San Quentin for a similar workshop, to be attended by a committee of model prisoners who are trying to create some productive projects for inmates. The committee has been meeting regularly but needs guidance.

"Can you handle this, Judy?" asked Martin, the Foundation director.

Hesitating briefly, I said, "Of course." I was still trying to prove my worth, and couldn't be seen as a wimp.

"Okay...let's schedule it for next week. That'll give you time to review their report, which contains some of their project ideas."

So here I am, inside San Quentin. As we enter the room, I see a group of eight men, notebooks in hand, sitting in metal chairs welded to the floor. They stare at me. My knees are shaking as I move to the front of the room. *What am I doing here?* I notice that the concrete walls have been painted a light grey, the steel door painted white. The room is brighter than the corridors I've been through, and has a single barred window high on the east wall. A wall clock is covered with a heavy plastic shield to prevent dismantling. The two guards remain with me as I reach the front desk, then move slowly to either side of the classroom, eyes on the prisoners.

Clearing my throat, I look out at my audience and introduce myself. I make eye contact with each man as the chairman introduces them. They are primarily African-American; large, muscled, tattooed, and very tough looking. They nod their heads as they hear their names, and are extremely polite to me.

"Okay, let's get started," I say. "We have a lot of information to cover today, and I want to be sure we have plenty of time for questions."

The hour-long workshop goes well. The men listen to my suggestions and instructions. They ask questions similar to those in many other workshops I've done.

"How do we know how much money to ask for?" asks a heavy-set, older man, a serious expression on his face.

"Don't worry about that," I say. "If our program execs like your ideas, they'll help you with that."

"My writing ain't so good," says the chairman shyly, looking down at the floor. "And I'm supposed to put this together."

"Hey, man," interrupts a lanky youth. "I'll help you. I was actually pretty good in my high school writing class."

"If you work together as a team, you can help each other. Besides, the Foundation is not looking for perfect grammar, but good potential projects."

"How long should our letter of intent be?" asks a short, stocky prisoner. "And how much detail should we include?"

"We don't dictate the length," I say. "Be detailed enough to make your project understood. Just remember to be as specific as you can, and include measurable desired results. Your projects have to have a purpose."

I listen to their ideas, which are good ones, ranging from new job skills training, an advanced furniture–finishing workshop, and a more comprehensive library for prisoners. They have many thoughts about ways to help prepare their fellow inmates for the "real world," such as training and practice for job interviews, information about technology, and reviews of banking and tax procedures. When the workshop ends, they clap their hands enthusiastically, commenting to one another in low voices as they shuffle to the wall to line up before marching back to their cells.

Before they leave, the inmate chairman thanks me and asks, "Why'd you come 'inside' to help us? Weren't you scared?"

"I came to help you with your ideas. Your proposed projects are just as good as any I've heard on the 'outside'. And, no, I'm not really scared."

Some of the men smile and elbow each other. Others look satisfied. I hope they will maintain their enthusiasm for their project ideas and get some support from the Foundation.

As I return to the entrance with my guards, I feel a surge of pride at what I've just accomplished. I am glad I came. I didn't show them my fear. When we reach the outer reception area and I look out at the bright blue sky and sunny day beyond, I feel an intense sense of my own freedom that I haven't known before. My experience "inside" suddenly makes me realize how much I appreciate my "outside" world.

Under the Redwoods

Under the Redwoods

Occupation

Christiane Diehnel

When I went out to play one morning in early summer of 1945, an astonishing sight greeted me. Rumbling down the street outside our apartment was a column of huge vehicles, all painted dark green. I remembered having seen similar ones many times before, but there was something different about these. The flags, which fluttered on top of each vehicle, were red, white, and blue with stripes and stars, instead of the black, white and red German flag. During the war, my parents had explained to me that those kinds of vehicles were military trucks and tanks with cannons mounted on top, which the soldiers used to shoot at the enemy in battles. They had looked very scary to me, and I had not liked them. There had been long columns of them moving through our city of Halberstadt in Germany at various times. I wondered why they had returned now, because I knew that the war had ended and soldiers were not shooting at each other anymore. I ran back to our apartment and called my mother, who came out with me to see what was so exciting.

"Those are American military trucks and tanks with American soldiers inside," she said. "They have won the war, and I think they may be here to occupy our part of the country. You don't have to be afraid of them, but be careful and don't go too close to the tanks so you won't get run over."

Christel, my best friend who lived in the building next door, had seen the trucks and tanks from her house too and came out to join me. We saw a few other kids and adults in the street looking just as curious as we were. The tanks were moving slowly down the street, and soon my mother went back to her chores with another reminder to us not to go too close to the big vehicles. Christel and I felt curious and a bit scared at the same time. Some of those vehicles had wheels taller than we were!

Just then, the column stopped, and we could see one of the drivers leaning out of a small window up high on a truck and waving to us. When his hand threw some candy on the street, Christel and I approached the truck and looked up to have a closer look. We saw a smiling face with very white teeth and very black skin. We had never seen anybody who looked like that. Perhaps the man's skin had been burned, I thought, but I was not sure. The driver called to us but we did not understand what he said. It sounded like a language we had never heard before. Christel and I looked at each other and were gripped by fear. We were even too scared to pick up the candy he had thrown down onto the street, and ran back home.

My mother explained to me that there were many kinds of people in this world whom we had not seen before, and some of them looked very different from us. She said that the soldiers in these vehicles came from America and some of them had dark skin because a long time ago their families had lived in a place called Africa where all the people had black skin. I still felt confused about the skin color and wondered where this place called Africa was, but my mother was busy and I did not ask more questions.

We found out that the Americans were just passing through our city, and soon we all got a taste of yet another segment of the human race. The advance contingents of the Russian occupational forces were Mongolian soldiers, who arrived in small wooden *panje* wagons pulled by ponies. The Mongols were short men with very black hair and slit eyes. They wore black tunic type uniforms. The ponies were small with long manes and tails. Two of them were pulling each cart. We could not understand the Mongolians' language either.

The decision on how to divide a defeated Germany had already been made by the three Allies, the United States, Britain, and the Soviet Union, during several meetings as early as 1943. France was included later on to become a partner of the allied powers and to occupy the part of Germany bordering their country after Germany had been defeated. The capital, Berlin, was to be divided into four sectors, each one to be occupied by one of the four Allies. Besides these arrangements, complicated agreements had been hammered out regarding eastern territories and countries annexed by the Hitler Regime. The final decision had been to keep Germany as an economic entity but not to allow a sovereign government.

During the summer of 1945, the German people lived in a state of confusion with a lot of uncertainty about the future. Not much information was available, and rumors continued to circulate.

Nobody was sure what would happen to our country, and how we were all going to survive. Besides that, we had not heard anything about the whereabouts of my father and my uncle Helmut, Tante Motte's husband, and did not know if they were alive or prisoners of war somewhere.

The arrival of the Mongol troops in our city sent shivers of fear through most women and made them hide in their homes as much as possible. When leaving our apartment, my grandmother made sure that her daughters wore shapeless old clothes, covered their heads with scarves, and avoided groups of these Mongols, who were rumored to have been sent by the Russian government to rape all the women in the city. We were very lucky that our family was spared this horror. My mother told me once that there were a number of close calls when she, Tante Motte, and Omi, were stopped on the street by soldiers who proposed in broken German, "Hey you, woman, I come visit tonight."

My mother always answered in a forceful voice while her knees were shaking, "You come tonight. My "boyfriend" is going to beat you. He is big and mean!" This imaginary boyfriend was a good deterrent. Many of the Russian soldiers did not like confrontations. Later on, after a typhoid epidemic had swept through our city, my mother and Tante Motte just had to mention that they had had typhoid fever to send the Russian soldiers running. However, for the moment my family continued to keep big kitchen knives close by our beds at night and hoped for the best.

I do not remember how long the Mongol troops stayed, but one day there was a long column of them leaving the city in their little wagons. Christel and I had been intrigued and had wandered over a block from our apartments to watch the departing Mongols. Our mothers were quite alarmed when they looked for us and found us near the Mongol troops. They were probably worried that we might be snatched and carried off to the Far East. Of course, this possibility had not occurred to Christel and me. We were only five years old and it seemed we still had a lot to learn. Our mothers reprimanded us and set strict boundaries for our wanderings.

The regular Russian soldiers who replaced the Mongolian ones harassed us in the same manner. Groups of them were always congregating on the streets, enjoying their never-ending supply of vodka. A black piano was still perched on the second floor of our bombed out apartment building and visible from the street. It seemed very appealing to some of the Russian soldiers to climb up there, especially after they had drunk vodka. My mother had forbidden me to climb up to the second floor where the piano was, and I was not to interact with any soldier going up there to investigate the piano. She did not want them to know that our apartment was occupied, and had said often that we would be safer if the Russians did not know that we were living in this building.

I understood some of what my family told me about being safe, and I tried not to get into trouble, but sometimes my urge to explore was greater than my mother's cautions. One day I heard piano music and I just had to check it out. I opened our apartment door quietly and stepped into the entry hall. The music seemed to come from the black piano perched on the second floor of our partially bombed out apartment building. I went to the door next to us where the music seemed the loudest and listened. I don't remember what was being played but it sounded to me like some of the classical music my family liked to listen to on the radio. After a few minutes, I decided I wanted to see who was playing piano and cautiously started to open the door.

Then, with a big crash, I fell backwards and found myself buried under the door, which had fallen on top of me. The heavy wooden door had just been leaning against the frame. My mother came running and pulled me out. There was blood all over the floor and on me, but the piano music continued undisturbed, the Russian soldier playing up there must not have heard anything. I had a big gash over my eye, which left me with a scar on my left eyebrow. My mother scolded me after she found out that I was not seriously hurt. She was probably more shook up than I was, and my grandmother had to comfort both of us.

Another one of the many incidents involving Russian soldiers stands out in my memory. We talked about it many times in later years, so I know all the details, which I did not quite understand at the time when I was five years old. One day, Herr Stein, the owner of our apartment building, knocked on our door. He was an older man and according to my mother not a hands-on, take-charge person. When my mother opened the door, he seemed quite upset and said, "Frau Benthien, you have to do something! There is a drunken Russian in the basement!"

My mother was puzzled and asked, "Herr Stein, that is not the first time a drunken Russian ends up in the basement. What do you want me to do?"

"Well," he said, "You have to get him out of there!"

"Herr Stein, it is your responsibility to do that. I am a woman and I have a small daughter. I am not strong enough, and if that soldier wakes up, I may be in trouble. No, no, you have to take care of him!"

"Frau Benthien, I don't know what to do, I have never had to deal with this kind of problem!"

"Herr Stein, you are a man, you can get this guy out of there!"

"But I am too scared. You do it!"

"No, I won't!" said my mother.

"Frau Benthien, please help me, you know better how to handle that, I don't know what to do, please!"

"Ok, Herr Stein, it seems that you are more scared than I am, so let us both go down there and see what is going on."

Cautiously they went down the stairs to the basement. The soldier was not moving, only snoring drunkenly. Who knows how he had gotten there. Herr Stein and my mother together dragged him up the stairs and deposited him on the street where they left him, still snoring. Our wimpy landlord was greatly relieved and left quickly.

This episode seemed relatively harmless in comparison to occasional nightly visits Russian soldiers paid us. Some of them must have found out that our apartment was occupied. Late one evening we heard voices, Russian voices, outside our apartment door followed by knocking and banging with rifles on our door, which had been barricaded with pieces of furniture as usual. It became clear that we had to open the door or the Russians were going to break it, perhaps even shoot their way in. My grandmother told my mother and Tante Motte to hide in the bedroom with me and not come out under any circumstances. She and my grandfather would handle everything.

My grandfather opened the door and found himself face to face with four Russians, each wielding a rifle in one hand and an open bottle of vodka in the other. One of them also carried a big sack. They demanded to come in and told my grandfather to get a woman to cook dinner for them. My brave grandmother stepped forward and was handed the sack, which contained potatoes, some meat, and cabbage.

One of the Russian said to my grandmother, "You, woman, cook food. We hungry, quick, quick!"

They all went into our small kitchen and watched my grandmother cook their food. The soldiers sang Russian songs while drinking and eating. Later, my grandparents said, the soldiers were polite and thanked them at the end of the meal, even leaving some food for my grandparents. Finally, they were so drunk that my grandparents managed to escort them out of the building and down the street where they continued to drink and sing. Could it be that these soldiers, far away from home, were just homesick and tired of living in military barracks? We endured several more occasions of having to cook dinner for Russians and every time my mother and her sister, knives in hand, would hover behind the locked bedroom door with me. They were ready to jump out and defend themselves, their parents, and me.

One time a "Russian visitor" politely asked Opi to use our bathroom, which was only partially functioning since we had no running water. Opi told the soldier to use some water from the bucket for flushing the toilet. We had to fetch all our water every day from a community water faucet, which had been rigged up on a street corner a few blocks away. We were very careful not to waste any of the precious water. The soldier spent a long time in the bathroom and my grandparents in the kitchen were getting concerned not knowing what was going on. His comrades laughed and one of them told my grandmother, "Mamuschka, you not worry. Friend in bathroom done soon."

When the soldier finally returned he seemed fine and all of them left.

My grandmother immediately went to check the bathroom and discovered that the soldier had not used the toilet but had changed into my grandfather's dirty underwear, which he had found in the laundry hamper. His own underwear was scattered on the floor. A close look told my grandmother that the soldier's underwear was crawling with lice! She let out a loud scream and then she and her daughters hurried to dispose of the lice by dumping all the clothes in the bathtub and pouring soapy water over them. That soldier must have been very itchy. We laughed about it many times in the years to come.

Under the Redwoods

Under the Redwoods

Mother's Kitchen

Donna Terdiman

She came back with my father and brother in the late afternoon of that gloomy day in March, 1994. They had been gone for the better part of the day signing the final papers for the sale of the house. During their absence, the packers had come. The movers were coming tomorrow. She was 87 years old. It was to be our last night in the house she had lived in for forty years.

When she stepped into the square front hall, she could have reassured herself that things didn't look all that different. In the living room to the right, the Steinway grand still stood in silent majesty along the picture window facing the street, its mahogany surface gleaming in what remained of the afternoon light. In the dining room to her left, the walnut French Provincial table and china cabinet remained in place. But her many paintings, as dear to her as anything she owned, had been crated that day. Her treasured collection of bone china teacups, the books, records, and photographs were now packed in cartons ready to move with her to California.

Under the Redwoods

My parents had spent nearly ten years wondering when to give up their home in Manhasset to live near their children, and several months anticipating the actual move. After an exhausting week of final decisions about what they could use in their small new apartment, what to give to family, now or later, and what to donate to the Salvation Army, my mother had come to terms with the things she was leaving behind. But not with the loss of her kitchen.

After checking out the rest of the house, she walked into the kitchen, not through the dining room, but down the narrow central hall of the house to what we jokingly called "the servants' entrance." Mother's kitchen was a large airy rectangle at the back of the house, its two windows and windowed Dutch door all overlooking the back patio and tree-filled back lawn. In 1954, it had represented the height of design.

It was now almost dark. In the fluorescent light of the overhead fixture, without the yellow warmth of the stove, sink and dinette lights, the beloved center of our house looked strangely cold and foreign. I quickly turned on all the lights I could. The green and yellow linoleum, patterned to look like tile, looked worn and dusty. The chipped ceramic sink, grubby from all the packing, still held the small stainless steel bowl filled with detergent and a sponge on a stick for cleaning the items that did not go in the dishwasher. I had convinced the packers that my mother needed to keep this bowl in place until the following morning.

The kitchen had Formica countertops of yellow-gold, all the rage in 1954. Topped by golden pine cabinets with dark hinges, they lined each of the long walls, and from the wall along the back of the house jutted forward to form a peninsula, and to separate the kitchen proper from the dinette.

A few items needed for breakfast in the morning remained on the counters and with my mother's detergent bowl, would be packed at the last minute: the kettle on mom's trusty gas stove, the toaster, the coffee pot and warmer. But the counters looked bare and neglected. I ran my hand over the smooth surface, thinking that we needed to run the sponge over it one last time. I had never noticed the many places where the metal edges had pulled away from the Formica. Already packed were the things that had given mother's kitchen its life, like the pre-war coffee grinder whose raucous noise and aroma of freshly ground beans – irresistible to me long before I learned to drink coffee – had always meant morning in my mother's house.

In the dinette, the wallpaper of ivy on a trellis, once fresh in green and white, now looked busy and shabby without the distraction of 40 years of kitchen clutter. Mother's round and clunky maple table, covered with an ancient gold oilcloth, and surrounded by six colonial chairs, still sat stuffed into the small space. The matching chest remained in place under the dinette window. On it, a tiny black and white television, kept alive over many years by my husband's electrical skills, would provide us with the news for the last time that evening and the following morning. The small bookcase of the same wood stood in the corner, but my mother's cookbooks had already been packed, as had the radio over which she had listened religiously to Carlton Fredericks preach about the evils of sugar, while her irreverent children made fun of the pretentious way he pronounced "pruunes."

My mother wandered through her kitchen distractedly, not touching anything. "I was very careful about telling the packers what to send to California, and what you wanted to give away, ma," I said gently, "and see, I made sure they left the detergent bowl so we can wash up the things we use for breakfast in the morning."

My dad came bustling into the kitchen, his eyes sparkling at the prospect of going out to eat. "I'm starving. Let's go to Louie's for dinner," he said. "What do ya say for some clams?"

My mother's eyes swept around her kitchen. "Why don't we just eat here tonight? I can make…"

"Ma," I interrupted, my stomach lurching, "we can't eat here. Everything's packed." I opened the doors to the empty cabinets to demonstrate, searching her face for signs of recognition that never again would she prepare a meal in the kitchen she had cooked in for 40 years.

Four months earlier, after putting on indefinite hold the idea of selling their house, my parents had called us with the news that a young family had made them an offer they had accepted. I found them a large apartment in a senior residence with lovely views of the Novato hills, but with no real kitchen. My mother would be able to prepare breakfast, but little else in her own apartment. My mother assured me that this would be fine with her. "I'm tired of cooking three meals a day. I will enjoy going to a dining room and being waited on."

"I don't believe that and neither do you," I said to her at the time. I reminded her that she had always preferred to eat in her own kitchen.

When I was a child, I used to complain to my mother that our house in Queens wasn't "fancy" like my friend Elaine's (pronounced "Ee-laine"). "Why don't we have a silk couch with curved legs, and lamps with fringed lampshades, and delicate tables filled with cute glass figurines?" I wanted to know why we didn't have a polished kitchen with shiny linoleum, and a glass top table, elegantly set with bright place mats for breakfast, lunch or dinner, and especially, "Why don't we go out for a chicken dinner every Sunday like Elaine's family does?"

"I like our house to be comfortable, not 'decorated'," was my mother's reply, "and I like to cook my own food." Even then I had to admit that her roast chicken was the best in the world.

Instead of going out for dinner, she preferred to have an informal open house on weekends, where old friends were welcome to come out to spend the afternoon talking, arguing politics, listening to music, lolling in the garden in good weather. Sometime in the late afternoon, my dad would serve gin and tonics for the adults, ginger ale for the kids, and my mom would prepare a simple and delicious meal, a pot roast or a leg of lamb, or her famous spaghetti sauce, learned from her friend Ruth LaGuardia who learned it from her Italian father-in-law.

Mom didn't feel isolated in the kitchen. The wonderful odors of braising or roasting meat and vegetables would draw her friends in to chat or help with chopping and preparing, and the sounds of "The Marriage of Figaro," or Beethoven's Seventh, or Bach's Goldberg Variations would sweep in from the hi-fi in the front hall. My job was cutting up the salad, unless, like Tom Sawyer painting his fence, I could hint to one of our guests how much fun it was to tear lettuce and cut up cucumbers, tomatoes and green onions.

Our family life centered around the kitchen table. My parents' house was large, able to accommodate relatives or friends from Montreal, Ontario, Boston or Baltimore, or points closer or further afield. Often relatives would arrive with little or no notice, and often friends coming from as close as New York City would stay the night. Whoever was there would help with the cooking and cleaning up. And whoever was there for however long, would gather around the kitchen table for gossip and discussion.

On that last evening in my mother's empty kitchen, I thought about all the toast and jam and boiled eggs for breakfast, the seductive smell of French toast and Canadian maple syrup for Sunday brunch, my father's late in life skill in frying eggs sunny side up, the only thing he ever learned how to cook. I thought about the discussions over the breakfast table about what was in the New York Times. "The real news is in the back pages among the furniture ads," my mother always maintained.

I thought about my grandmother's frequent visits from Montreal and her intense interest, to the end of her life, in what was going on in the world. "Why is Daddy yelling at Bubby?" I once asked my mom at the breakfast table.

"They're only discussing politics dear. Don't worry, Bubby is not taking it personally. Besides, she can hold her own." My father had strong political beliefs, and needed to vent his rage at whoever disagreed with him, mother-in-law, friend or Joseph Alsop, of the New York Times, whom my dad liked to call "All-slop." His rants passed quickly, like a summer storm, and he never retained grudges, except for Joseph Alsop.

I remembered my mother's lunches of sardines, or of cottage cheese, sour cream, nuts and raisins, or anything else that was in the refrigerator. I remembered her belief in protein at every meal and whole milk for growing girls. I remembered sitting around the kitchen table with my friend Margaret eating cherry-vanilla ice cream and quizzing my parents about the New Deal.

I remembered the delicious smell of my mother's pot roast, carrots and potatoes braising on the stove. I tried to estimate how many times I had cut up the salad on that now defunct Formica peninsula. I remembered the first time Joe, despite having a terrible cold, devoured my mother's pot roast and noodles. "He really enjoys food," said my mother. "He'll make a good husband." At one of our first visits after our marriage, Joe sat down at the kitchen table to copy out the recipe he named "mother-in-law noodles."

I remembered the joy at each of the visits of my mother's sisters and families from Canada with fresh supplies of Cadbury's biscuits, and Robertson's jam, Marmalade for my mother, Wild Brambleberry for me, and most important of all, Red Rose tea. After the hugs and kisses the first thing we did when anyone arrived or was about to leave was to gather in the kitchen for a cup of tea. We used to joke that our home was prepared at any time for the emergency delivery of a baby, because my mother's kettle was always on the boil. She liked her tea piping hot.

I remembered the many visits with my own family to grandma and grandpa's house. As children, David and Cindy loved the big brick house with the stairs, the yard, the ping-pong table and the tricycle in the basement, and grandma's mashed potatoes and carrots. I remembered the stories and games with grandma and grandpa around the kitchen table.

On that last night, I remembered two frantic grandmothers as babysitters trying to get six week old shrieking Cindy to accept her first bottle when all Cindy wanted was the milk from her mother's bursting breast. I remembered the bliss all of us felt when I finally came home and nursed her at the kitchen table. Cindy gazed intently at me, her huge dark eyes still filled with tears, and sucked with enormous efficiency and satisfaction. Grandma Florence and grandma Sarah almost sobbed with relief, while the men, grandpa Joe, daddy Joe and two year old David looked on in wonder.

As I stood in the empty kitchen that last night, I remembered my father at the sink, with one of my mother's aprons around his ample middle, doing the dishes and loading the dishwasher as only he knew how to do it. And I could picture a younger version of my mother in the midst of preparing a meal, leaning over the counter to laugh and share a story, or parading dramatically around the kitchen to describe a play or opera she had seen.

On that last night, we were eventually able to convince mom that her kitchen was no longer functional and she agreed to go to Louie's for dinner. But beneath the noisy talk about how much we would miss the cherrystone clams, was the comprehension of a much deeper loss for my mother and for all of us. There was no way to transport my mother's kitchen to California.

She is gone now, as is my dad. The Steinway dominates my living-dining room now, along with the china cabinet and the English tea cups. Her paintings are in every room of my house, and in my children's houses. She never did a painting of her kitchen, but part of it is with me. I can't replicate the wonderful smells of my mother's cooking, but I have her cookbooks and recipes. I still make a variant of her spaghetti sauce – only occasionally, since we don't eat much red meat, and of course, "mother-in-law noodles."

My California house is nothing like hers, but I like to have informal groups of people over, and they are always underfoot in my large kitchen. I love it when my cousins or good friends come to visit and we can prepare and share meals, talk and laughter. My children grew up discussing art, ideas, books and politics over the kitchen table.

I have my parent's pre-war coffee grinder, although we make much better coffee than they ever did. I like to use her plain brown teapot, her Corningware, her bowls, and several of her pots. People often comment on my peculiar habit of keeping a small stainless steel bowl of dishwashing detergent in my sink. And I make a salad every night.

Under the Redwoods

Lost

Where in the hell did I put my plot?
I've looked everywhere.
It's the only plot I've got.
Maybe it's in the Frigidaire
Don't laugh
Last week I found my glasses there.

The damned adjectives are everywhere
Leaping around like kangaroos
Shrieking "pick me, pick me!"
They've even gotten into the garden
And are driving the flowers crazy.

Where, oh where is my plot?
Why is it always plot I haven't got?
Even those elusive verbs
Always hiding in the dictionary
pop out now and then saying
"Find me if you can!"
then duck back in again.

Under the Redwoods

Metaphors float around like balloons
And then the similes come out to play with them
Confusing everything
Cliches are a dime a dozen
I can find them any old day
But my plot, I have not got!

Adverbs gaily play up on the ceiling
Until the Queen of Tarts arrives
Off with their LY's she cries
And they slowly dribble down
But they don't find my plot
The plot I have not got

The house has become chaotic
All the words bounding around, no order to be found
Even the prepositions and conjunctions
Have found fertile ground
And are causing trouble.
I may have to become despotic
Call a meeting amid the rubble and say
This is a situation up with which I will not put!
Now where in the hell have you got . . . My Plot!

Anne Sisler Latta

Under the Redwoods

Memory Police

parked
in the back of my
brain

waiting to ticket
me
if I forget
too much

traffic tickets
missing keys
blank names

of those I know
well
files misplaced

objects that
disappear
for no reason
at all

major accident
total forget
memory police
take my brain away

Janet Wentworth

Decisions, Decisions

Nancy Dods

I sat at the end of the breakfast table looking out the wall of windows at the breaking of spring. Walt was opposite me, Suzie and Laura to my left, and my son Walter to my right. Since the kids had reached their teens and were busy with after-school sports and jobs, breakfast had become our family time together. Most mornings there was animated conversation; however, this morning everyone was rather quiet.

I looked at Walt, dressed in his business suit, soon to leave for his job in San Francisco. I looked at the girls in their uniforms, ready to be driven to Upper Lucas Valley where they then would walk over the hills to San Domenico School. I looked at Walter, skinny as a rail, wolfing down his breakfast, eager to dash up the street to pick up his friend Rich , and devour another day of life in elementary school. My day loomed ahead.

Gosh, it was mind boggling. Should I do the laundry, or sweep the yard, or grocery shop? How about dusting or maybe even clean the bathroom, or vacuum? My choices were many.

"I could have been a doctor if I hadn't married you," a voice said.

Four heads looked up. Three stared blankly at the source, me; one looked puzzled and a trifle hurt.

Since I had been a little girl, my dream had been to be a doctor like my grandfather, my aunt and two uncles. I had held that dream until I met chemistry. Slowly the dream faded. I settled for zoology and then was married, became a mother, and happily enjoyed both.

Here I was, 36 years old, in 1975 at the beginning of women's lib, harboring some (some?) discontent. One of my classmates was Prime Minister of Belgium; another was an author, others were lawyers, vets, doctors, educators and one a college president. My day looked really bleak in comparison.

"Why don't you go to medical school then?" Walt responded.

My eyes had been welling up in self-pity. I sniffed and wiped my eyes with the back of my hand. I hadn't expected that. I didn't know what I expected, but certainly not that kind of encouragement.

The children were still looking at me blankly. They kept on eating.

Breakfast ended in more silence. Everyone pushed back, scurried to gather his or her backpacks, coats, briefcase, lunch. I kissed Walt goodbye, then Walter. The girls and I got into the squareback and drove to the drop-off point. (Some days there was a bull in the field. On those days I dropped them off and drove quickly away so I wouldn't see them get trampled. They never were.)

When I got home I sat down and tried to figure out why I had blurted that out and what I hoped to accomplish by it. What kept coming back to me was the "gathering scenario." Picture a room filled with friends and strangers. You visit with those you know, then strike up a conversation with a stranger. The conversation is going well; he (usually) is listening to your thoughts, philosophy, ideas, theories. We are having an adult conversation.

"By the way," I say, extending my hand, "my name is Nancy Dods."

"Oh, I apologize. My name is John Fletcher," he replies, squeezing my hand tightly.

We continue our conversation, then he says, offhandedly, "What do you do?"

I pause. What do I do? I started the San Francisco Suicide Prevention Auxiliary. I edit a newsletter for the Wellesley Club and the San Francisco Junior League. I solicit jobs for underprivileged teens at corporations so they can get on-the-job training. I teach nature study and woodworking at San Domenico. But it is all volunteer. It isn't a job.

"I'm a homemaker," I answer.

As I'm standing there, I can see the eyes glaze over; I can see the smile fade. The eyes dart around the room. Then I hear the inevitable.

"Excuse me, will you? I'm going to get (fill in the blank – another glass of wine, something to eat, Oh, there's ------)" and he is gone.

It seemed as if a person's worth was valued by a paycheck; no paycheck, not worthy. Was I trying to fulfill a dream, or was I trying to establish my worth? How many pre-med courses would I have to take before I could even submit an application to a med school? I thought of the hours of studying required, the time away from my family. I thought and thought and thought, for days and days and days. I talked to Walt. He stressed the positive aspects. I struggled. One day I was convinced it was the right thing to do, and the next day I was filled with doubts. You can imagine what a joy I was to live with!

I continued to do what I had to do, all the while thinking, vacillating, looking for the answer. It came to me on Mission Avenue in San Rafael in front of Falkirk. Like a cartoon balloon, my mind was filled with the realization that this dream was a dream whose time had passed. I wasn't giving up the dream; I just wasn't up for it. Realistically I knew that (1) I didn't want to spend all the necessary time studying, and (2) I'd probably throw up the sight of all the blood I'd see. At the same time I acknowledged that, as blasphemous as it was for that time, I liked being a homemaker.

I knew what Atlas would have felt like had he been reprieved. I felt free, great, happy! From that day on, I felt as if I were the luckiest person in the world. I got up every morning knowing I could do WHATEVER I WANTED TO. If it were a beautiful day, I could work in the garden, go for a run, sit outside and read. If it were cold and dreary, I could cook a stew and bake a pie, so that the house was filled with welcoming aromas when everyone came home. I could go to my children's sporting events. I could meet Walt in the city for lunch. I could do all these things because I wanted to and not because I had to.

I learned first-hand that happiness is worth much more than a paycheck.

Chap's Guitar Music

Janet Wentworth

The first time Chap pulled his guitar case down from the passenger overhead as we flew over the mountains of Mexico I was embarrassed. I thought, "Oh no! ...he isn't going to break into song on this silent plane right now? Couldn't he at least wait until we get to Zihuatenejo?" I watched as he pulled his guitar out of the case and shuddered as he burst into song: "*Hay! Jalisco, Jalisco, Jalisco, Tu Tienes, tu novia, Ques Guadalajara.*" Apprehensively, I glanced around the tourist-packed Mexico Airlines plane and noticed a few astonished, and un-smiling faces as this gray haired, Ivy league type in a traditional cotton plaid jacket burst into Mariachi song. By the second stanza of *Jalisco, Jalisco, Jalisco*, I saw relaxed smiles. By the third stanza, the American tourists were swaying to the music, including me.

We were headed for Mexico City where we were to meet Chap's brother, Straff, and his wife Marion before going on to be Straff's guest at his Hotel Catalina in Zihautanejo. We had just become engaged – the third time for both of us.

Later, on the moonlit beach in Zihautenejo, Chap entertained American and Canadian guests with his guitar: *Besame Mucho, Peregrina,* (a haunting love song about an American journalist who fell in love with a Mexican General), and *Jalisco.*

The vacationers sang along until 1 a.m. with Chap's American classics: *I Believe, As Time Goes By, Spanish Eyes, Fascination* and *You Made Me Love You* – among others.

This first trip to Mexico with Chap was my introduction to 25 years of the magic of my New England husband's mariachi guitar south of the border.

Whiskey Max

Anne Sisler Latta

"Whiskey Max." I read the name on the ornately carved wooden marker. "Kind of a bizarre name for a rose bush, don't you think, Tazz?" My Golden Retriever stared at the bush, then at me. Of course, he agreed.

"Well, anyway, Whiskey Max, you're going to be moved to the other garden. Hope you're ready."

I pushed the shovel into the dirt, doing my best to uproot the old rose without too much damage. After a few minutes I threw the shovel down and sprawled on the grass. Tazz sprawled next to me. We'd been moving plants since dawn and needed a rest.

"Don't stop digging! Get me out of here!"

I sat up. Tazz sat up, cocked his head, and stared at Whiskey Max.

"Did you hear that, Tazz?" By now Tazz was on his feet, tail wagging, nose close to the ground by Whiskey Max, whining with excitement.

"Of course he heard it," said the voice. "Dogs hear everything.

Now dig me up."

"Oh, my God! Not only do I talk to animals and plants, but now they're talking back to me!"

"I am not a plant," the voice said with indignation. "I am a woman, and I've been buried under this damned rose for years. Now get me out of here."

"I have to call the police. I can't dig up a body."

"I'm in a jar, perfectly safe for you. My daughter put me here. Now dig me up!"

By this time Tazz was running around in excited circles giving me imploring looks. Then he began to dig to China under Whiskey Max, dirt flying backwards from frantic forepaws.

"Okay, okay." I picked up the shovel and went to work too.

"Dog's smarter than you are," grumbled the voice.

"Don't be a wise ass or I'll leave you down there," I said.

There was a clink as my shovel hit something. On my hands and knees I unearthed the most extraordinary urn – its surface gleamed with iridescent blue crystalline flowers.

"Thank you, God," said the voice with a big sigh. "I never wanted to be buried."

"Who *are* you?" I asked.

"Who are *you*?" said the cranky woman's voice.

"I own this house. This is my garden."

"Well, I *used to* own this house, and this was *my* garden."

"What are you doing here now?" I asked.

"My daughter planted me here after I was cremated. She kept me in the bloody damned garage for a long time, stuck in between the fungicide and the bone meal – didn't know what to do with me or maybe she just wanted to torture me. She'd come out from time to time and shake me. "How're you doing in there, Mom?" And then, just for spite, she planted me under this rose, Whiskey Max. Can you imagine – me, a teetotaler, planted under a bush called Whiskey Max! She was supposed to scatter my ashes in Yosemite, but she never did do anything I asked her to do. Children!"

Tazz and I sat back on our haunches, too stunned to respond, staring at the glistening blue urn. Tazz looked at me as if to say, "What now?"

"Where in Yosemite?" I asked finally.

"There's a great meadow just south of the Ahwahnee Hotel where you can see Yosemite Falls and Half Dome and all the way west down the valley." Her cranky voice became dreamy. "That's where I want to go. But," she added, "not too close to the Merced. Don't want to be washed down to Modesto. God, what a thought – the rest of eternity in Modesto!"

"Do you know what's weird?" I asked, letting out my breath.

"Weirder than talking to an urn?"

"You've described exactly where I want to be scattered. I've told my family and friends this many times in almost exactly the same words."

"Great minds think alike." The voice paused for a moment. "Would *you* take me there?"

Tazz pushed his nose up against me, nudging me, tail wagging, and let out a few woofs. He loved to ride in the car.

I thought for a moment. "Why not," I said. "I love Yosemite."

"Well, let's get on with it then."

"Don't be so bossy, or I'll put you back in the garage, this time right next to the slug bait," I said as I set her urn on the kitchen counter.

Tazz's toes clickety-clacked on the floor as he followed me from room to room while I threw things in a duffle bag for our impromptu trip. The lady in the urn was silent except for an occasional exaggerated sigh of impatience until we got to the car.

"I'd like to ride in the front seat up where I can see."

"See? How can you see? You're in an urn, and if I may say so, you're not exactly in one piece."

"I can sense things – it's even better than seeing, actually."

I arranged her on a box and brought the seat belt across her urn, snugging her in.

"Oh, this is just fine," she said. "Now, drive down I 5 and turn left at Gustine."

Tazz hopped into the back of the wagon, rested his chin on the top of the seat back, and clamped his gaze on us, his brown eyes moving back and forth from me to her as if watching a tennis ball.

"I think I should at least know your name if I'm taking you all the way to Yosemite to scatter you."

"Clarissa. It's Clarissa."

"Are you, uh, or rather, were you, very old?"

"Born in 1892, died in 1976 or thereabouts."

"Well, you couldn't have always lived in my house."

"*My* house. Well, no, I was born in Bellingham, Washington. Grew up in a log cabin in the woods. I remember the walls were covered with newspapers. Helped keep out the cold and you always had something to read."

"My sister lived in Bellingham," I said. "She called it 'boring Bellingham.'"

"I called it 'beautiful Bellingham'. All my folks were from there. My first husband too."

"Your *first* husband?"

"Yes. He came from the richest family in town – paper mill. His family thought I was from the wrong side of the tracks." She snorted. "Couldn't tell it by behavior, though. I divorced him."

"Divorced? That must have been around the time of World War I. Wow! I didn't think people *got* divorced in those days."

"The Great War. It wasn't easy, but the doctor told me I was lucky I didn't have some disease given the way that fool husband of mine played around. He was such a handsome man though, and I surely did love him. Terrible time. Everyone upset. But I wasn't just going to sit there and pretend everything was hunky dory. No sir, so I took my two girls and moved to Chicago. Got a job as a secretary for the Milwaukee Railroad."

By now we had reached Gustine, I had turned left as directed and we were headed east for the Sierra.

"It's hard enough being a 'single mom' today," I said. "I can't imagine what it was like in those days."

"Wasn't easy. During the depression, too. I remember my girls would arrange their dates at different times. One would go out in their only dress and have to get back in time for her sister to hop into the same dress to go out with her own date." She laughed. "It was hard, but we had fun, too."

"Did you marry again?"

"Yes, praise the Lord, to the kindest man you've ever known."

"What was his name?"

"Orville, so of course we called him Sam. He was an attorney for the Milwaukee railroad. In fact, I was his secretary. We had to wait, though, until he got divorced."

"You had an affair with your married boss? You are some hot babe."

"Can't help who you fall in love with. If the rocks in your head fit the holes in his, well, there you have it."

"How'd your daughters take this?"

"They loved him. Only father they ever really knew. The oldest married another attorney from the railroad. Had a real broom up his 'you know what' he did. They had four kids."

"And the other one?"

"Ah, the one who buried me under Whiskey Max? Always trouble, that one. Hollywood beautiful and funny. How she could make us all laugh. She married a naval officer. Sam and I just loved him." She paused, then sighed. "I hate to talk about this part. He was a sub skipper in the Pacific during the war. Came home safe. My daughter was pregnant with twins. They'd already had a little girl in 1940 and were hoping for a boy. For the first time, I saw my daughter truly happy. Then he was killed in a car accident coming home from his boat's decommissioning. My daughter never got over it. I tried to help her. Traveled all over the world, wherever she was to help her with the children, with her terrible second marriage. In the end, I had to accept that her life was up to her. I could do nothing. Pray for her. Love her. Let her go. After I died it didn't take long before all the smoking and drinking caught up with her. She died much too young, but I think she wanted to."

We fell silent, the lady in the urn and I. We passed through fields of sandy-gray grass where some ancient muscular giant under the earth had heaved shards of jagged rocks through the surface. We wound through Mariposa and along the Merced River. Her words had found their way to that raw place inside of me like water finds its way through crevices in rock.

"There's nothing you can do either, dear," she said after a while. "You have to let him go, somehow."

"What do you mean?"

"Your son. You have to let him go. He's choosing his own path."

"How in the world could you know this?"

"I sense great sadness in you. Oh, you cover it up by being a smarty and a wiseacre, but I feel it. I recognize it. Children can bring such sweet sorrow. I've sometimes thought the pain of childbirth is just to tip us off as to what's coming next."

"I've never felt more helpless," I said. "Angry too."

"Well, when you think about it, we brought them into the world, we're responsible for their being here. We carried them around for nine months after all, before they even popped out. It's agony to watch them suffer and know you can't do a damned thing about it. And motherhood lasts forever."

"How do you bear it?" I asked.

"You just do."

In silence we passed under Arch Rock, the granite monoliths which guard the entrance to Yosemite like giant sentries.

"Whenever I pass beneath these rocks I half expect to hear a voice booming out 'All who enter here are blessed,'" I said.

"Amen," whispered the voice beside me.

We drove along the gorge of the Merced, its white sheets of water bounding over boulders.

"What if I kept you?" I said.

"What do you mean, kept me?"

"I could put you on the mantle and we could talk."

"Are you crazy? Are you going to become that batty old lady who talks to an urn? Don't you think your friends would notice?"

"I talk to my dog, don't I?"

"Well, keep talking to *him*. Dogs are great listeners for the most part, except for addle-brained beagles or those little fuzzy things that yap. I'd be bored silly sitting on your mantle listening to you prattle on."

"It was just an idea."

"Well, get another one!"

I parked along the side of the road and we sat for a moment staring at Half Dome and listening to Yosemite Falls flinging itself down the cliffs. Green meadows spread toward the river.

"Shall we go?" she said.

Tazz hopped out of the back and I put him on leash. We unbuckled Clarissa from her perch.

"God's cathedral," she sighed. "I can almost smell the air."

"I really don't want to do this now. Why can't I keep you for just a little longer?"

"Because it's time for you to let go, honey. Besides, I've *got* to go. I want to be free of earth."

So, Tazz and I walked her to the middle of the meadow.

"Go on, *do* it, dammit!"

I opened the urn and Clarissa's cinders rose, weightless, glistening on an invisible breeze like so much confetti.

The ribbon of her voice curled down to me. "Thank you," she called.

Tazz and I walked to the bridge, sat on the bench and watched the setting sun send its sheen up the river to our feet.

Under the Redwoods

Turning Points in My Life

last turning point
reality of age
enjoy life now
near future
Poof! and I am history

early turning point
I was born
my parents turning point
Poof! I'm an adult

young & pretty
career of sorts
fall in love
Poof! I'm a mother

three turning points
vying for love & attention
divorce their father
Poof! a single working mother

fall in love again
another dear turning point
divorce her father
Poof! a single working mother

Under the Redwoods

fall in love again
this one forever
until he dies

Poof! retired, widow
grandmother

my life in retrospect
a movie in fast forward

new turning point

write about it
Under the Redwoods
Writing Group
ups and downs

tragedy & joy
success & failure
condensed

prose & poetry
pages & sentences
scattered thru
our computers

Under the Redwoods

Poof! where's our book

"write before writing
it's in your head"
the pundits say

"the law of delay
one of the great
forces of nature"

"there must be time
seeds of thoughts
memories
to be nurtured
in the mind"

for better writing
one published author used
the word **wait**

waiting and writing
feedback
from under the redwoods

Poof! here is our book

Janet Wentworth

About the Authors

Christiane Diehnel

I grew up in Germany and came to the United States in 1961 when I was in my early 20s. After living in San Francisco for a while, I met my husband, Roger, who grew up in Oregon. We settled in Marin County where our two sons were born. Mark and Derek liked to hear my war stories, i.e. my experiences during WWII as a young child. Eventually they suggested I write it all down because they would not be able to remember the details. I also write about my many adventures becoming part of a remote village community in the Amazon Rainforest in Peru. I hope that will be another book.

Nancy Dods

I was born in Excelsior, Minnesota, in 1938. My family lived there until I was eight years old, at which time we moved to Kansas City, Missouri. That was home until I went to college at Wellesley. There I met my husband, Walter, who was studying at Harvard. We were married in 1959 and have three children: Suzie, 52; Laura, 50; and Walter Junior, 46. We have lived in Marin almost 48 years. During that time I have been an active community volunteer for many organizations. I have been a part of our writing group, which evolved from Jackie Kudler's class, *Tales Told from Memory*, since its inception.

Judy Storey Edgar

One thread that weaves my life experiences together is my passion for education. I have pursued this as a student at Wellesley and Cornell, as a mid-life graduate student at Golden Gate University, as a teacher, classroom volunteer, college trustee, and as a board member of several educational non-profits. For me, a highlight was my role in 1981 as a founder of Marin Education Fund, now 10,000 Degrees, a college access and financial aid organization in which I am still involved.

Born and raised in New Jersey, I lived in New York, Delaware and Michigan before settling in Marin County 42 years ago. My years working in the field of philanthropy with the San Francisco Foundation, the Buck Trust, and as an independent consultant, provided much material for writing my stories. I have always hoped to have the time to write, and now I finally do. My husband Jim and I have three adult children, three grown grandchildren, and three very young great-grandsons.

Anne Sisler Latta

I've had at least twenty lives in this life time. Each one is often related to where I lived at the time – Napa Valley, Philippines, North Carolina, Florida, Paris, Seville, New York City, and finally Marin County in various incarnations as student, traveler, wife, mother, feminist, sailor, real estate agent, perennial student of French, and grandmother, all glued together by family, friends and memories.

There have been life-altering experiences along the way – mind-opening studies at college, bumming around Europe for over a year in my 20's, living in France, Spain and New York City, giving birth, reading Betty Friedan's *The Feminine Mystique*, fighting for the Equal Rights Amendment, having a career, unexpected deaths, and the wonderful gift of my grandson for whom life is a "cabinet of curiosities," as it is for me.

Donna Terdiman

I grew up on Long Island, studied at Mount Holyoke, graduated from Barnard College and the Columbia University School of Social Work in New York City, and came over the rainbow to Marin with my young family 44 years ago.

Stories have been central to my life, first as a reader, later as lover of theater, student of history, and professionally, as a social worker. I still love to puzzle over the meaning of narrative, in all its forms. Not until first taking Jackie's writing class in 2002, did I face the irony that in many ways I knew more about English history than my own. My son and daughter had long told me that they didn't need to know as much as I did about the English kings, but were really interested in what had directly shaped their lives. I have greatly enjoyed exploring their past and mine in writing my own stories.

Janet Wentworth

It matters to me I was born
Not when
I started life as Hervor Bruce
And will end this life as
Janet Wentworth

Under the Redwoods

A full life
For what it is worth
Three husbands
Four children/one lost
A lot of magic
A lot of tragic

Started writing in the 40's
Fashion copy/ad agency
Vogue magazine/Newsletters
Public Relations/Radio spots

I learned a little about real writing
From my third husband
A newspaper publisher
He edited my weekly columns
Coaxed me through deadlines
Encouraged every phrase

Now he is gone
I'm taking classes
Learning to write stories
From my basement files
As a fourth generation San Franciscan